HELP, MY BODY IS KILLING ME

Solving the Connections of Autoimmune Disease to Thyroid Problems, Fibromyalgia, Infertility, Anxiety, Depression, ADD/ADHD and More

Dr. Kevin Conners

authorHOUSE®

AuthorHouse™
1663 Liberty Drive
Bloomington, IN 47403
www.authorhouse.com
Phone: 1-800-839-8640

© 2010 Dr. Kevin Conners. All rights reserved.

No part of this book may be reproduced, stored in a retrieval system, or transmitted by any means without the written permission of the author.

First published by AuthorHouse   10/27/2010

ISBN: 978-1-4520-8509-8 (hc)
ISBN: 978-1-4520-8510-4 (sc)
ISBN: 978-1-4520-8511-1 (e)

Printed in the United States of America

This book is printed on acid-free paper.

Because of the dynamic nature of the Internet, any Web addresses or links contained in this book may have changed since publication and may no longer be valid. The views expressed in this work are solely those of the author and do not necessarily reflect the views of the publisher, and the publisher hereby disclaims any responsibility for them.

Introduction

I believe we serve a sovereign God and he has ordained everyone for distinct purposes. One of mine is to share hope to those who are at the 'end of their rope'. Those suffering from autoimmune disorders seem to be the outcast of the medical community since they have no real answers to offer them. If you find yourself in that category, I hope this book changes that for you. If you Google Auto-Immune disease, you'll find that it is a process where your body is destroying its own tissue. There tends to be an unnecessary mystery around auto-immune disorders and like many named diagnoses, we are sometimes lead to believe they are curses we have inherited from our ancestors or unexplainable phenomena that have no known cure. I will try to refute such myths and shed a bit of light on disease in general so that the average person on the street may better understand management of their own condition.

Autoimmune diseases in general are commonly overlooked in both traditional medicine and alternative healthcare. This is at least in part due to the fact that neither traditional medicine nor the alternative model of care has had much, if any, success in treating them. If we look at the traditional model of care, we find that complete immune suppression is the treatment of choice; its success rate is horrible and the patient is often killed by the medications meant to help them. Alternative solutions have fared better only as far as they didn't kill the patient.

In 25 years of practice, I've seen the failings of both models and have experienced my share of disappointments in attempting to give patients a fuller life. Quite simply, both models do not work. In my quest to find a solution for the tremendous suffering that autoimmune conditions bring upon their victims, I first had to admit that what I was doing just did not work. It was so frustrating; my brain could not rest and my mind would not be at ease. Though I take no credit of my own in the methods of correction this book will lay out, I am ecstatic over the hundreds of patients I have been able to help since discovering the solution. The "solution" to treating patients with autoimmune disease lies in understanding the mechanism. The mechanism assumes knowledge of biochemistry, anatomy, physiology and neurology. I simply stand on the shoulders of the many far more intellectual than I who have paved the way to help those in need. My hope is that this book brings true HOPE to those who have suffered too long!

In this book you'll find patient testimonials scattered throughout. I changed the names for obvious reasons, but these are just a few of the stories we hear on a daily basis. We have six, three-ring binders full of 'success stories', so many that we stopped asking for them about 2 years ago. Believe me when I say that there IS HOPE. Don't ever give up! If you are sick and in pain, call me personally, I am always open for consultations. God led you to this for a reason; you need to believe!

My prayer is for you,
Dr. Kevin Conners
651.739.1248
www.UpperRoomWellnessCenter.com

Chapter One

Identifying Mechanisms

"Even in literature and art, no man who bothers about originality will ever be original: whereas if you simply try to tell the truth (without caring twopence how often it has been told before) you will, nine times out of ten, become original without ever having noticed it."
                                                                    C. S. Lewis

Anna's Story

At 47 years of age, Anna thought her life was going to get a little easier. As the mother of three boys, crazy days were the norm throughout the toddler and school years. Now Tom, her youngest, just graduated from High School and was to be leaving for college in the fall. Though Anna had been secretly fanaticizing about going back to school, getting a job she'd enjoy, or just taking up painting again, a hobby she enjoyed 'before kids', she now wonders if she'll be able to do anything at all. Just a few months before Tom graduated, Anna started getting severe knee pain that started in the right leg and soon became bilateral. She passed it off as stiffness from non-use until it grew in intensity and both knees swelled for no apparent reason. After her medical doctor prescribed 800mg of Advil to be taken every four hours, she grew suspicious that there was little attempt to discover the cause. *The pain and swelling worsened and Anna was referred to a rheumatologist who, after some testing, diagnosed her with Rheumatoid Arthritis. Anna was devastated and her prognosis seemed grim – medications for life to simply 'manage' the condition.*

One of the things that happened over time, in traditional medicine, is that their model for care has become governed by whether there exists pharmaceutical intervention. The purpose in obtaining a diagnosis is simply to administer medications to manage the symptoms. They may look at autoimmune conditions and believe that as long as they give the condition a Latin name, the investigation is over and they simply need to open the Merck Manual and prescribe the appropriate drug. If the person has Rheumatoid Arthritis, let's try Tramadol, if the diagnosis is Multiple Sclerosis, our protocol may be Interferon; if the person is hypothyroid, we're going for replacement hormones, and at first we don't succeed, then try, try again.

Success is measured by the suppression of symptoms not correcting the cause that is producing an effect. The population seems to be okay with this model: Give my symptoms a name and then drug them into oblivion. Unfortunately, we are going to discover that this type of mentality is leading us down the road of destruction. The question they really need to ask is why they became sick in the first place. The answer to this question for many suffering people may lie in the fact that they have an immune destruction against their tissue that, unless stopped, is continuously progressing and may ultimately cause death. We cannot be satisfied with symptom suppression while ignoring the cause; we must never settle for a treatment that does not address the reason the disease exists; and we must become our own advocates, studying and demanding that our healthcare practitioner 'proves' their cure with logical understanding of the process itself.

Robert's Story

He was only eight years old when he was diagnosed with Type 1 Diabetes. He's been on insulin injections for 23 years now and has a difficult time keeping his blood glucose levels perfect, with frequent spikes and drops. That's not what brought him to seek help though. Four years ago his energy was going through extreme hills and valleys. His wife questioned him about stress at work and they frequently fought over things that 'bothered him' that previously were never an issue in their 9 years of marriage. Robert refused to go to counseling but did agree to a visit to the family doctor. After a routine blood workup revealed nothing out of the normal range, his MD ordered a TSH, the test for the Thyroid Stimulating Hormone. In traditional medicine approaches, the TSH alone is run to determine the health of the thyroid gland. Sure enough, Robert's TSH was 47, more than 40 points above normal and it gave the doctor what he wanted – a diagnosis! Robert was diagnosed with low thyroid and placed on synthetic thyroid medication for life.

Robert's story is identical to the millions of other 'hypothyroid' patients. Typically, when people do have a hypothyroid response, they generally don't really feel that much better with replacement after what I call the "honeymoon period". Their TSH's look really nice and pretty with lab work but in reality, the patient does NO better, even if symptoms are subtly suppressed. They still have NOT addressed the cause of their condition and if you don't fix the cause, the disease progresses! We'll discuss the fact that hypothyroidism is NOT really a disease of the thyroid at all but an autoimmune attack on the thyroid from a normal functioning immune response that has 'gone awry'. We will discuss why that takes place.

We also have to be fair and address how hypothyroidism has been traditionally supported from an alternative medicine model. In Robert's case, after two and a half years of dissatisfaction in the replacement model of care through his MD, he decided to take the advice of a friend and visit a Naturopath. The naturopathic doctor gave Robert iodine and tyrosine supplements and a glandular product to support the thyroid in an attempt to give the gland the building blocks to recover. As was true in Robert's case, these usually don't do anything to correct the cause of the problem because they do NOT dampen the immune response against the thyroid. It is equally a failing approach and will often do less for the patient's symptoms than replacement therapy.

If there is any 'take away' from this book may it be to stimulate the reader to ask one simple question as to their symptoms – "why?" If the answer to your question leads you to believe you may have an autoimmune disorder, don't stop asking and don't accept any treatment that isn't logically treating the answers to your constant questions of, "Why?" When we see a person that has an autoimmune disease of any name, the goal really is to discover the cause (the reason 'why') of the immune dysregulation and make every effort to correct that. If you don't support and modulate your immune system you will NEVER improve your physiology and the disease will simply progress to complete destruction and then begin to attack other organs and systems.

In the case of autoimmune disease against a specific organ like Hashimoto's hypothyroidism, there is little help in direct organ support without correcting the cause. The mechanism for the issue is the immune response in the first place and not that the organ is deficient in any type of nutrient; the reason the person may need hormone replacement (such as Sytheroid) in hypothyroidism is because the immune system is actually destroying the cells, but replacement without halting the destruction is missing the point. Both approaches are like throwing a sandwich to a man being attacked by a pack of wolves; even if your intent was to help him, he has bigger problems than hunger.

When we look at a person that is not well, one of the first questions needs to be, "what's the mechanism". One of the main mechanisms is an autoimmune mechanism, and we'll talk about how to test for antibodies, and to follow these up with immune panels and specific antigen testing to discover the cause.

Both approaches are like throwing a sandwich to a man being attacked by a pack of wolves; even if your intent was to help him, he has bigger problems than hunger.

Let's face it, if either traditional medical or the alternative models had any great percentage of success treating autoimmune disease, you wouldn't be reading this book. Robert understood that it was "reasonable" that failure to discover the cause of thyroid destruction would lead to further destruction. He also saw that it was "reasonable" that someone 'out there' must be able to find out what was causing the destruction; and he thought that it was "reasonable" that if whatever was at cause for such destruction could be evaded, then it was "reasonable" that the destruction would at least slow down. He also reasoned that this deductive thought process would yield him success. Robert was a 'man with a mission' and his hard work and refusal to 'own his disease' led him to find the answers that would change his life forever!

When we look at any thyroid loss of function, we know that the metabolic rate of the person will decrease over time. We know that thyroid hormones have very powerful effects on controlling the metabolism which enables the body to attain homeostasis – a balance of health. This is why when people are truly hypothyroid, their cellular metabolic rate decreases, they cannot produce the energy in the mitochondria and they have a very hard time attaining a balance in their well-being; their response to viruses and bacteria may diminish, they struggle recovering after stress, just don't feel as well as they used to and have very low energy. Many of these symptoms come on gradually and if the person is in their thirties or older when the attack takes its hold, they often chock it up to symptoms of aging.

We also know that when a person has thyroid problems they have a diminished gastrointestinal motility, with sluggish gastrointestinal tracts, and they're often diagnosed with deficiencies in digestive enzymes when the reality is that the body doesn't have enough metabolic capacity to move food along so there's fermentation, bloating, gas and constipation. This leads to re-absorption of intestinal toxins and intestinal permeability. This problem is true for many other autoimmune conditions, since many end up attacking parasympathetic nervous centers in the brain that control peristaltic motion.

Another common lab finding with all autoimmune conditions and most certainly in Hashimoto's patients is that their serum gastrin levels are low. This is an obvious sign of hypochlorhydria or a deceased production of hydrochloric acid in the stomach. There exist strict influences between loss of thyroid activity and gut function.

We also know that when people are autoimmune, several anemias become more probable for developing. One of them is the microcytic hypochromic anemia associated with iron deficiency. Many times when people have low thyroid function, they become iron anemic because they lose ability to absorb iron (and a variety of other nutrients) due to the gut connection listed above. Their slowed intestinal motility has irritated the absorption sites in the small intestines and decreased the ability of enzyme reactions necessary in bringing these nutrients across the gut wall. The decreased intestinal motility also breeds biological attacks in the gut where opportunistic organisms take advantage of static food sources and wreak havoc. The decreased movement of fecal matter also leads to leaks in the gut membranes and systemic infections that remain 'low-grade' and sub-clinical. Then, to make matters worse, because their metabolic rates are down, these people don't respond well to iron supplements and they often bring about further constipation and misery. What a mess!

Another type of anemia that is common with autoimmune patients are the normocytic-normochromic anemias. This is when the hemoglobin, hematocrit, and RBC levels are depressed but the MCV, MCH and MCHC are normal. Many things can cause normocytic-normochromic anemia, but one of the possibilities is always autoimmune disorder.

Pernicious anemia is an autoimmune attack against a chemical called Intrinsic Factor which is the agent personally responsible for the absorption of vitamin B12. It is not uncommon to see someone that has one autoimmune condition and pernicious anemia, another named autoimmune disease at the same time since the diagnosis of autoimmune disease is named after the organ it is attacking, and the attack has no end if the treatment is centered on suppressing symptoms.

How would the lab panels look to a traditional medical or alternative doctor that doesn't understand that they are really dealing with an autoimmune mechanism: they diagnose the patient with primary hypothyroidism and B12 deficiency – thinking that they are dealing with two, separate and distinct disease processes. Though the next step should be to look for Intrinsic Factor antibodies along with thyroid antibodies, this step is often skipped yet, would be the telltale sign of an autoimmune response. Treatment with oral doses of B12 doesn't work well if the problem is a lack of functioning Intrinsic Factor and if your doctor is thorough and re-tests to discover the B12 'deficiency' still exists, B12 injections may be in order. This may solve the problem of the low lab tests for B12 but has done NOTHING for the autoimmune attack on Intrinsic Factor and the stomach where it is produced let alone the thyroid. So the cycle of chasing symptoms continues!

It is important to understand that an autoimmune disease is a 'state' that the immune system is in. It is NOT a disease of an organ; and even though it is given a multitude of names depending on the tissue currently affected, it is a STATE of the immune system attacking the tissue it was meant to protect.

We also know that when people have low thyroid activity, Insulin Growth Factor 1 (IGF1) levels seem to drop. We know that the hypothalamus-pituitary axis releases this Growth Hormone; that's the part of the brain loop with the pituitary gland, also know as the 'master gland' since it stimulates so many other hormonal systems. Growth Hormone generated from the production of Insulin Growth Factor 1 then has all the positive anabolic effects on the physiological systems that we attribute to Growth Hormone such as youthful energy, slowed aging, faster healing and everything good about being young. So, when people have autoimmune conditions, they age faster, seem to lose energy quickly, they can't recover after workouts if they still have the ability to force themselves to do such, and they just don't feel well in general. Of course, they could probably find some 'doctor' to administer Growth Hormone injections for a price.

Another expression of autoimmune processes and Hashimoto's altered thyroid activity involves neurotransmitter production and expression of the neurotransmitters epinephrine and norepinephrine. These are made in the adrenal glands that sit right above each kidney. They are another part of that hypothalamus-pituitary axis we spoke of. A change in the normal rhythm of release of the adrenals will eventually lead to depression, anxiety, and swings between the two. This leads to a struggle with the ability to handle emotional stress, process and sort consequences in difficult circumstances, etc. These integral expressions of the Frontal Lobe's Pre-Frontal Cortex are dependant on neurotransmitter function. A decreased stimulation of these processes combined with a diminished oxygenation due to the iron anemia previously discussed is a vicious cycle that spirals the patient downwards. Though appropriate Brain Based therapies are beneficial for the firing into the neuronal centers, the inflammatory process must be stopped. We give these patients named diagnosises like ADD, ADHD, anxiety, depression, OCD and the likes.

The neurotransmitters that are typically involved here are epinephrine and norepinephrine but the secondary effects of Frontal Lobe function ultimately involves a more complex down-regulation of other neurotransmitter production centers and the patient slides downhill. Not only is there a decreased production but there is a decrease in the systemic function through a loss of sensitivity. It's also a part of the reason that some hypothyroid patients have difficulty losing weight and why ADD, ADHD, anxiety and depression patients can't control their moods. Epinephrine and norepinephrine stimulate lipolysis, the breakdown of fats and aid in Frontal Lobe expression. When one loses the responsiveness of these neurotransmitters, they have a very hard time burning body fat despite the fact they may work out and exercise and consume far less calories than their workout partner. Discouragement sets in, combined with sloppy neurotransmitter receptivity in the frontal lobes, the patient often ends up on anti-depressants, chasing more symptoms and never addressing the cause. Again, never stop asking, "Why?"

Other things that are found with autoimmune processes are decreased hepatic (liver) and biliary (gallbladder and bile ducts) clearance. When we look at the detoxification pathways of the body we understand there exists Phase I and Phase II pathway. Both these phases are highly nutrient dependant and the Gastro-Intestinal disturbances, decreased gut motility, and decreased absorption rates in the autoimmune patient decreases the ability for them to do the very thing they NEED to get better – Detoxify!

Many have said, "You are what you eat." More appropriately, "you are what you absorb." Since one absorbs both nutrients and toxins through skin and through the lungs, diet is not the only way one might absorb vicious poisons. An even more appropriate statement might be, "You are what you do NOT detoxify!" Since the process of detoxification is taking place on a constant basis through these Phase I and Phase II pathways in the liver, it is what one CAN'T detoxify that becomes a part of us and makes us sick.

The purpose of these pathways may be simplified as the liver taking non-soluble solutions and chemicals and converting them to water soluble components that can then be expelled through the digestive tract, the urinary system, the skin via sweat, and the lungs. Problems come in with autoimmune disorders. Phase II conjugating enzymes can't mature in autoimmune disorders and the detoxification potential over a period of time will be compromised. Compromise the detoxification pathways and the chance of the patient ridding them of the antigen that is causing this entire reaction goes down exponentially.

If we understand Hashimoto's Disease, we can understand every autoimmune reaction. So what is autoimmune thyroid? Autoimmune thyroid disease is typically classified into two groups, Hashimoto and Graves'. Both Hashimoto's and Graves' can cause a hyper, or an overactive thyroid response, but it is Graves Disease that is dangerously overactive thyroid and Hashimoto's that hovers low.

When someone has an overactive thyroid their blood testing will indicate a low Thyroid Stimulating Hormone (TSH) and a high T4 and/or T3. These people typically have increased metabolic rates, symptoms like high anxiety, nervousness, insomnia, and heart palpitations, racing heart, and inward trembling. Though these symptoms may also be similar to a hyperactive adrenal state, both a Graves and a Hashimoto patient may experience these symptoms.

The difference between Hashimoto's and Graves' is that Graves Disease always expresses itself as hyperthyroidism and Hashimoto's patients are more typically hypothyroid; though they can experience some hyperthyroid symptoms like those listed above, more often those symptoms stem from subsequent adrenal dysfunction happening concurrently. Hashimoto's patients ultimately experience hypothyroid symptoms which we have and will discuss in more detail.

Unfortunately, in the current healthcare system, these people typically don't get evaluated from an autoimmune perspective, which may be a hidden blessing since the traditional medical approach to autoimmune disorders is currently quite barbaric. Hashimoto's disease is far more common than Graves but both are autoimmune, i.e., caused by an immune attack against the tissue; they just have different outcomes. If you can understand the mechanism of the Hashimoto's immune attack, then you can equate much of it to all autoimmune disorders.

Hashimoto's is the most common cause for hypothyroidism in the United States and has been published and well accepted in the endocrinology literature, but often overlooked in traditional and alternative healthcare models as far as applications. In the alternative medicine model, hypothyroidism is blamed on things like iodine and tyrosine deficiencies and need for thyroid glandulars and though this has been our approach for quite some time, we really have not seen much success in this treatment. The traditional medical approach is hormone replacement. Neither model addresses the attack on the thyroid tissue and both are destined for disaster.

As in all autoimmune conditions, there is tissue destruction in Hashimoto's; the reason their thyroid is not working is because their immune system is attacking the gland.

We first need to address the mechanism involved. All autoimmune diseases may have some type of genotypic component, i.e., there may be a latent gene that the individual has carried in an unexpressed state for a period of years until some 'event' that triggered a immune response suddenly 'turned on' the gene. If this exists, and the autoimmune disease truly has genetic components, the practitioner's job is to rightly manage the patient to diminish the immune response and calming the attack. Once a gene is expressed, it will always stay 'turned on'. We will walk you through procedures to keep it 'calmed down' to stop the destruction mode. Other processes can 'turn on' an autoimmune attack like environmental compounds, some types of endocrine imbalance, toxic chemical exposures, abnormal stress responses, antigen responses, as well as the person's preexisting genotype. So, the combination of all these things and some genetic susceptibility leads to an autoimmune disorder.

Usually the immune system is slowly attacking the tissue over several years. And then, the person eventually has a great enough destruction that brings about symptoms that lead them to seek some type of doctor. In the case of Hashimoto's, they often get diagnosed with hypothyroidism because their TSH is high. And then, the TSH is managed by replacement but no management for the immune response is initiated because it was never assessed. In the case of other autoimmune disorders, the patient is often misdiagnosed for years, even decades; and they are left laden with multitudes of drugs attempting to suppress their symptoms.

The autoimmune response is an inflammatory response, which produces chemicals called cytokines, which are part of the body's natural defense system against outside invaders. The body's immune system may be separated into a Th1 and a Th2 response. The Th1 response may be thought of as the police force, the body's initial strike force against an invader or what is called an antigen. When an antigen is present, the Th1 system fires and kills the virus; should the bug be of a nasty persuasion and strong enough to resist the Th1 response, the Th2 system kicks in, creates antibodies against the virus, tagging them so appropriate white blood cells can finish them off. A person with an autoimmune disease has this process stuck in the 'on' position, either hyper-Th1 or hyper-Th2, which prolonged, destroys the tissue where the antigen is recognized.

In Hashimoto's, if the autoimmune disorder is hyper-Th1, certain types of lymphocytes and cytokines become 'dominant'. This is an inflammatory, destructive response. These cytokines also block thyroid receptor sites from creating a proteomic response thereby making the hormone that is present, unresponsive; well, that stinks, even the hormone that IS present works worse! So, even when thyroid hormones bind to the receptor site, the actual proteins that impact metabolic rates are not produced rendering it inactive. This is why Hashimoto's patients, despite the fact they go on replacement, don't necessarily feel better after the 'honeymoon' period of a few weeks to several years because there's a defect created from the inflammatory immune response blocking the ability for the replacement hormones to have an effect on the receptor sites. This is why simply replacing the absent hormone doesn't work!

Hence, both the traditional medical and the traditional alternative models of care are doomed to failure. The most important battle to fight is to calm down their immune response and stop the destruction.

The "new model" we are proposing is simply to be more specific. If an autoimmune disease is a hyper-Th1 or hyper-Th2 attack against an antigen, doesn't it make sense to do everything possible to find out what the antigen is, attempt to remove it and calm down the Th1 or Th2 dominance? I'm no rocket scientist, but this makes sense to me. It's logical and possible to find the specific biochemical pattern perpetrating the response so we can determine how we treat them.

Angela's Story

Angela, a seventeen year old senior in high school has suffered her share of teenaged teasing. She started gaining weight in sixth grade and no matter what she has done to stop the process, the pounds have been adding up. Her mother and she have been in Weight Watchers 3 times, she's tried Jenny Craig, joined a gym and even joined the school's cross-country team, all leaving her discouraged, exhausted, and shamed. She has learned to live with her problem and excels in mathematics. She hopes to be a teacher some day. Angela's parents are divorced and her mother partly blames her failed marriage on her daughter's weight problems. She has taken Angela to the medical doctor but the simple and incomplete blood tests performed were "normal" and more shame was piled onto the heap of a stressed physiology.

Midway through her senior year, Angela's mother was referred to a functional medicine doctor who ran a more complete thyroid panel, including TSH, T4, T3, reverseT3, T3 uptake, and thyroid antibodies. Suspecting an Autoimmune thyroid from the symptoms alone, the doctor also ordered a fecal parasitological test and stool and gene testing for soy, gluten, egg, casein, and yeast. The testing was expensive but the doctor seemed confident and Angela and her mother were ecstatic just to find someone who would take a thorough assessment of her situation.

It's cases like this where I tell my patients that we HOPE something in the tests come back positive. We need to know what is going on in order to treat the patient. Discovery, the preparation before the battle, is the secret to winning the battle. While I was in college and professional school, I 'earned a living' painting houses over the summer. I'd walk door-to-door in the older neighborhoods of the sleepy, rural, river town I grew up in and asked homeowners if they needed any painting done. I was never short of work; one hundred year old houses are in constant need of repair. I learned quickly that to do the job right did not mean I needed to just slap some paint on the chipping lapboard. There were at least a dozen coats of color over that four inch siding and preparation for a new coat would be the biggest battle. It was the preparation that was the hardest work. Scraping aged paint down to smooth wood bloodied my knuckles and cramped my fingers. It didn't take more than one under-bid job to realize that the preparation was going to take much longer than anticipated and cost me more than time.

I learned much from my summers of painting that equates to treating autoimmune conditions. Preparation is more than half the battle – you have to spend the time and money to discover the cause of the disorder. Dig until you find the gold!

Luckily for Angela, she found a doctor who never gave up. Her thyroid antibody test came back negative, which would indicate to most doctors that she was NOT autoimmune. But he knew that if she was autoimmune, Th1 dominant, her hyper-firing Th1 system would be suppressing the Th2 antibody production – she still may be a Hashimoto's patient, the digging didn't stop. Specific cytokine testing was ordered while they waited for the results of the stool antigen and gene tests. Sure enough, Th1 cytokines were elevated and a CD4:CD8 ratio was imbalanced; Angela is suffering from an autoimmune disease! That week the stool testing results came back and at least one antigen was identified – Angela was autoimmune gluten! She carried two gluten genes and they were both expressed (turned-on).

Finally some answers. A detailed plan of elimination, detoxification, and Th1/Th2 immune regulation could be undergone. Angela's doctor (and new best friend) made sure that further testing to determine the effect on other tissue was done so he could support every down-regulated system to give her the most comprehensive support possible and the greatest chance of success.

Angela and her mother had similar questions, concerns, and frustrations regarding their problem that we see from most patients: "Why didn't my doctor test for this?" "Why wouldn't anyone else believe me?" Believe me when I say that we've even had patients take their test results back to their primary care doctors to be told that they are crazy and the problem is all in their head. I've seen doctors even have the gall to write them a prescription for Prozac on the spot. What is wrong with these people!? It's like a painter slapping another coat of paint over chipping wood – it will look good at a distance but just another example of shoddy work.

Common Symptoms

Although there are numerous different named autoimmune diseases, each with its own unique symptoms depending on the tissues being attacked, autoimmune diseases do share some common characteristics. The following core characteristics are experienced by the majority of sufferers of autoimmune disease symptoms:

Extreme Fatigue - Or, the kind of fatigue that is not alleviated by rest. This is experienced almost universally by autoimmune disease sufferers.

Muscle and Joint Pain - Whether it is general pain, burning, aching and soreness in the muscles or joint pain or aches, this symptom can also be found in almost every autoimmune disease.

Muscle Weakness - Feeling weak, particularly in the muscles, and loss of hand or arm or leg /thigh strength is a common symptom.

Swollen Glands - These can be all over the body, but especially in the throat area, under the arms, and at the top of the legs in the groin area.

Inflammation - Inflammation is a part of every autoimmune disorder. The warning sign of pain, especially when chronic, is a sign that something needs immediate attention.

Susceptibility to Infections - Frequent colds, bladder infections, ear infections, sore throat, sinus problems and yeast infections are common, with a slower recovery time, for people with autoimmune diseases.

Sleep Disturbances - Difficulty falling asleep and/or frequent waking is experienced by almost everyone with an autoimmune disorder.

Weight Loss or Gain - Changes in weight, typically in the 10 to 15 pound range, is often a sign of numerous autoimmune diseases.
Low Blood Sugar – Dysglycemia is also a sign of adrenal fatigue, common in many autoimmune disorders.

Blood Pressure Changes - Most autoimmune people have low blood pressure, though some have high blood pressure. Some experience feelings or dizziness or vertigo, fainting, palpitations and fluctuations in heart rate.

Candida Yeast Infections - Virtually all autoimmune diseases have gastrointestinal issues in common. Candida infestations, chronic parasitic infections, and H. Pylori infections may manifest as digestive disturbances, sinus infections, vaginal yeast infections or thrush.

Allergies - Many people with autoimmune disorders have numerous extreme food, chemical and environmental allergies and sensitivities.

Digestive Problems - Abdominal pain, bloating, tenderness, heartburn, cramps, constipation, diarrhea and excessive gas (looks like you're three months pregnant) reflect a condition known as "leaky gut syndrome", common with many autoimmune diseases.

Anxiety and Depression - Mood and emotional changes, panic attacks and excessive irritability are common symptoms in most autoimmune conditions.

Memory Problems - Often known as "brain fog", is a common autoimmune disease symptom that appears in most conditions.

Thyroid Problems - Many people have hypothyroidism, though some are hyperthyroid. Often this does not show up on a typical thyroid test and may manifest as low body temperature, a decreased metabolic rate, headache, chronic fatigue, cold hands and feet, inability to lose weight and excessive hair loss. There is a much longer list than this that a thyroid patient may exhibit.

Re-Current Headaches - Can manifest as migraines or severe headaches in some people.

Low Grade Fevers - This is very common, with some people experiencing this every day.

Pre-menstrual Syndrome - Autoimmune disease symptoms often increase around the menstrual cycle. Extreme bloating, painful cramps, heavy bleeding and irregular cycle are common.

Re-Current Miscarriage - This is a very common symptom in many autoimmune diseases.

Perimenopausal Symptoms – Hot flashes, sweating and fatigue are common with women going through their change of life but this is not normal.

As you can see, this is NOT an extensive list of autoimmune disease symptoms and it may be hard to believe that these symptoms are in any way connected. You are probably not experiencing all of these symptoms (at least we hope not), but if you are experiencing many of them, you're not alone.

We believe that more and more people are realizing that there is a connection between their various symptoms and illnesses, and this is the theory that is followed by most health specialists studying autoimmune disorders. Unfortunately, many medical professionals still treat the body like it is a conglomeration of separate symptoms, which is not working out too well for many autoimmune disease patients. We are not saying this to criticize the medical community; we are simply stating a fact. We strongly believe that the symptoms of any autoimmune disease affect the whole body, and consequently the body needs to be treated as a whole.

My opinion is that all chronic health patients should be tested for autoimmune disease. If the testing reveals such an attack, the battle is to figure out a way to dampen their immune activity. That is why it's necessary to do all the testing and select the most sensitive tests. "My doctor already tested me for gluten and he said it's not positive…" "But I had a H. pylori test already…" The blood test for gluten and H pylori are highly unreliable and reveal a lot of false negatives. You need to do the Enterlab stool and gene profile for gluten and the Urea Breathe Test for H. Pylori. New, more sensitive testing is being developed all the time; find a functional medicine doctor who is spending the time it takes to keep up on current trends. Immune panels need to be run with their Th1/Th2 cytokine breakdowns, a complete CBC with 1, 25 Vitamin D and 25 Vitamin D testing; get Homocystene levels, B-12 and a lipid panel. Always keep on digging and search for every possible antigen – there is often more than one!

Suzanne's story

"My mother died at age 56 from cancer. She had Cushing's disease as a young woman and had surgery on her adrenal gland. Later she developed hypothyroidism and was on replacement hormones for that since I was a little

girl. When she was diagnosed with breast cancer, she tried everything to get better; she had surgery to remove the tumor and at the same time they removed several lymph nodes. She did just as her doctor said; she was always that way. She went through chemotherapy and radiation and just got sicker and sicker. It wasn't until about two weeks before she passed that she told me that she thinks she probably made a mistake. 'I should have followed my own intuition,' she said. You see, she became convinced that they were all connected, the cancer and the hormonal problems. The more I learn about autoimmune disorders, I am sure that her intuition was right. When I was diagnosed with hypothyroid at age 34, it was after my mother's death and I made the decision there that I was NOT going to go the same route she did. I'll admit, it took a lot of searching to find a doctor to treat me differently but it was worth the effort. I don't want to get cancer; I don't want the same fate as my mom, and I feel that I'm on exactly the right path. Autoimmune diseases can run in families but how you treat them makes all the difference in the results you will experience."

For a doctor to rely on TSH alone or TSH with T4 and T3 alone in diagnosing and monitoring thyroid treatment is just mismanagement. TSH levels can vary greatly from day-to-day making it completely unreliable for treatment plan assessment; and this variation in TSH levels can happen without any treatment whatsoever.

So, in people with Hashimoto's, their TSH will go up and down, up and down, up and down, unrelated to any treatment because when the immune cells are attacking the thyroid, there's the release of thyroid hormones in their bloodstream and that release of thyroid hormones into the bloodstream then suppresses their TSH. So, depending on which day you test the patient, they may look like they have a normal thyroid.

This is how improper testing leaves a patient misdiagnosed, mismanaged, and just plain miserable! YOU have to take responsibility for your own health and find a doctor who will work with you until the answers are discovered. There is always a cause to an effect, always a reason for a symptom; there is always a reason 'why', you just haven't yet found someone to help you figure it out.

Rick's Story

Rick was diagnosed with Rheumatoid Arthritis in Spring 2005 at 39 years old after many years of doctor visits with different symptoms, mainly joint pain that moved from joint to joint with some episodes lasting weeks, others months. He was very confused and angry, being an athlete in high school and college; this pain was now interfering with life goals. What he had learned was heartbreaking enough for him. The three words he noticed to be associated with Rheumatoid Arthritis in whatever he read about it at that point were **"incurable", "deformation", and "progressive".**

Like many men, Rick went into denial and kept his diagnosis to himself. He quietly started on the medication his Rheumatologist prescribed but it made him feel nauseous and he slowly weaned himself off of them without returning to his specialist. He lived his life avoiding some of the things he loved most until one day in 2006 when his right knee swelled up to the size of a grapefruit. It was then that he decided to figure out an answer that would defy those three nasty words that rang through his head. Rick was driven by fear. He was a successful businessman and convinced that he was the one who cared most about HIS disease and if there was to be an answer found, then HE was the one to find it.

After finding a naturopathic practitioner who listed Rheumatoid Arthritis in her website with the immune system's mechanism laid out in clear language, Rick started to 'see the light'. He was on a plane the following week to start a process that would change his future for the better.

For Rick, it was, "Just common sense, I was between a rock and a hard place, I was really in a catch 22. I worked my whole life to enjoy golf, tennis, and living in my retirement years and all I could see was progressive, deforming arthritis or horrible side effects of drugs that didn't even help very much. I mean… maybe they work for some people but I just felt stuck. It forced me to do my own search."

The immune system is made up of white blood cells which make our neutrophils, monocytes, basophils, eosinophils, and lymphocytes. And when you look at the CBC on a blood panel, you'll see just the percentage of all these cells, your total white blood cells, neutrophils, monocytes, basophils, eosinophils, and lymphocytes. Those markers alone are not enough to help you understand what's going on in an autoimmune attack.

Many times, in the breakdown of these white blood cells, these markers or percentages may be totally normal. In order to assess an autoimmune disease, you have to do a lymphocyte panel – a separation of these into their various components.

The lymphocyte panel will measure the total percentage of T cells, the total percentage of T helper cells, regulatory cells, suppressor cells, cytotoxic T cells, B cells, and natural killer cells. Then, you can get a better idea of what's going on with the immune response in how it is responding to destroy foreign invaders, i.e. antigens.

When an antigen comes into the body, a macrophage, the Th1 response, will attack it. When the macrophage attacks it, it releases a cytokine called interleukin-1. Interleukin-1 then stimulates T helper cells which call for back-up. The back up arrives as Natural Killer Cells and T Cells and should they not be able to muscle the invader to the ground, they call for help to B cells, the Th2 response. The messengers involved in the Th2 response, which are used to make antibodies, are things like interleukin-4 and interleukin-10.

When the antigen is recognized, the macrophage that's present in the tissue in which the antigen infiltrated will attach to it and release interleukin-1. Interleukin-1 stimulates T helper cells and T helper cells then send out the cytokines to both the T cells and B cells to trigger cell-mediated Th1 attack within the cell and then a humoral-mediated antibody B cell response to try to really destroy the antigen. And this is an active Th1-Th2 response.

Over a period of time, the antigen is destroyed by these immune cells and then the immune response is supposed to stop with the activation of T suppressor cells. T suppressor cells then become elevated and the immune response is halted and balance is restored.

When we look at an autoimmune disease, the antigen that initiates this normal process infiltrates the tissue in question. The body recognizes the antigen and the immune response begins in an attempt to destroy the invader. But what if the invader is stubborn? What if it's developed an uncanny ability to wall itself off and prevent its own death? What if the antigen is not a living organism? If it's not even a living organism, can it die? This immune response is meant to combat virus, bacteria, fungus, molds, yeasts, and other living, parasitic, opportunistic beasts attempting to colonize in a host. What if the police force is dealing with a robot that doesn't die when struck by a bullet? Chemicals, toxic metals, exogenous hormones, food proteins, and environmental poisons are just a few possible antigens that may be the driving force behind an autoimmune response. We HAVE to find the mechanism of the immune attack.

Another marker we can use for autoimmune patients is the CD4/CD8 ratio, CD4 being T helper cells and CD8 being T suppressor cells. If a patient has an elevated CD4/CD8 ratio above 2.0, the immune response is in the 'drive mode'. Through treatment, we can see if we're actually effective in managing their immune response if we look at this CD4/CD8 ratio, and you see it drop from let's say 6.0 down to 4.0. We know we are moving in the right direction.

It's absolutely necessary to figure out if a person is Th1 or Th2 dominant because it will dictate what type of nutraceutical protocols that will be most effective for dampening their immune activity. We know that typical 'immune stimulants' like Astragalus, Echinacea, Garlic, Glycyrrhizin, Melissa Officinalis, Maitake mushrooms, seem to stimulate the Th1 response. We also know that things like pine bark extract, grape seed extract, green tea extract, Pycnogenol, Resveratrol, and caffeine are things that stimulate the Th2 response. So if a patient's autoimmune attack of their joints in Rheumatoid Arthritis, thyroid in Hashimoto's, myelin sheath in Multiple Sclerosis, etc., is a Th1 dominant response, adding Th1 stimulants will MAKE THEM WORSE! You can effectively aid in balancing a Th1 dominant individual by giving Th2 stimulants and visa, versa.

Vanessa's Story

Thirteen years ago Vanessa was diagnosed with Systemic Lupus Erythematosus (SLE) or Lupus for short. Her problems began long before her diagnosis after the birth of her first child, Ashley, when she was just 18 years old. Lupus is defined as a chronic, inflammatory autoimmune disease. It frequently affects the skin, joints, kidneys, but, like autoimmune diseases do, it affects multiple organs. Symptoms vary from person to person, and may come and go. Since autoimmune diseases are either a hyper-firing Th1 or Th2 response, it is when that system is most active that the person experiences the most symptoms. This is why patient's symptoms seem to wax and wane. The condition may affect one organ or body system at first and then progress to involve others. Almost all people with SLE have joint pain, arthritis and chronic fatigue. The joint pain is usually in the fluid filled joints like the fingers, knees, and hips. These joints have joint capsules which are sacs made up of essential fatty acids, prone to accept antigens and therefore common attacks of the immune response. Vanessa's youth was troubled; both her father and mother were alcoholics and Vanessa ran away from home at age 16. She bounced in and out of relationships, got pregnant at age 17 and was unwelcome in an attempt to return home. She had her baby while living at a shelter. Her increased stress, use of experimental drugs, emotional depression and the accompanying fluctuations that pregnancy brings the Th1/Th2 immune response may all have been contributors to the autoimmune 'switch' being turned on. Her symptoms have gradually gotten worse over time and even though God intervened in Vanessa's life when she got saved at a youth rally when Ashley was just 5 months old and she now is happily married, the disease has progressed.

Once an autoimmune disease has turned on, there is no turning it off. Traditional medicine had given Vanessa little hope and just prescriptions to fill. She tried multiple medications with some relief but different side effects. It wasn't until she found care with a functional medicine doctor who understood the autoimmune process that she began to take the upper hand against her disease. "It was the first time I ever understood what Lupus was," she commented, "I thought I was just doomed with a genetic disease that I'd have to live with the rest of my life. The last 3 months since starting care has been remarkable. I feel like I have a new life."

Vanessa's story is commonplace. Autoimmune patients feel helpless and hopeless; they have basically been given a death sentence by modern medicine with no alternative but symptom suppressant drugs. There is hope, and if you just keep digging and asking better and more pointed questions, you can find the answers; but you just might have to ask different people.

Sometimes the patient's history will be obvious as to which dominance they are 'stuck' in. If they've attempted taking high amounts of Garlic and Echinacea only to feel horribly worse afterward, there's a pretty good chance they are Th1 dominant autoimmune. If drinking green tea or coffee takes away the pain of your Gout, the possibility exists that you are Th1 dominant; if it made you feel worse, you may be Th2 dominant. But do NOT rely on this; it is always wise to do the testing!

You have to be very careful stimulating a Th1 or Th2 response. People can't figure out why they still feel terrible even while taking the boatload of vitamins their nutritionist recommended. If you are stimulating the dominant, hyper-firing system, you are literally throwing fuel on the fire. Autoimmune patients CANNOT take supplements that have both Th1 and Th2 stimulants. You are helping the immune system destroy your body! Do the testing!

One of our office handouts:

Th1 and Th2 Balancing

There are 2 parts of your immune system, the Th1 and Th2 response. When a person is autoimmune, one of these systems is "hyper-firing" or Dominant. Balancing this system goes far in reducing a patient's symptoms:

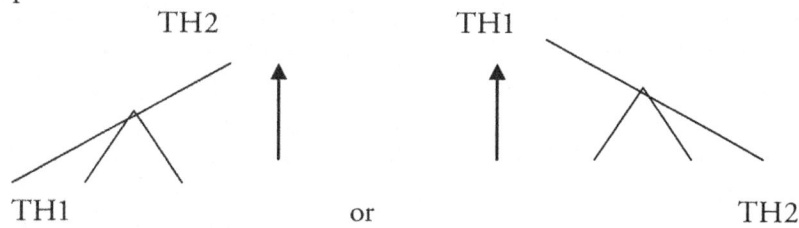

TH2 Dominance   TH1 Dominance

These SHOULD be balanced!

There are specific dietary changes and supplements that can help and hinder the above response: NOTE: ALL AI cases need Vitamin D, Glutathione, and Omega 3 fish oils +

Things that stimulate the Th1 response: (Take these if you are Th2 Dominant)

- Echinacea
- Garlic
- Vitamin C
- Immune stimulants
- Licorice root (Glycyrrhizin)
- Astragalus
- Beta-glucan mushroom
- Maitake mushroom (Grifola frondosa)
- Lemon Balm (Melissa officinalis)

Things that stimulate the Th2 response: (Take these if you are Th1 Dominant)

- Caffeine (don't add this as this does a number on your adrenals)

Green Tea
Grape Seed Extract
Herbal barks (Cramp Bark, Pine Bark, and White Willow Bark)
Lycopene
Resveratrol
Pycnogenol

Therefore, if a patient is Th1 Dominant, they should AVOID Th1 Stimulants and may TAKE Th2 Stimulants

Pregnancy is a common trigger for autoimmune disease. Autoimmune disorders can get triggered with surges of estrogens that take place postpartum. We also know that surges of estrogens like birth control pills can sometimes promote the onset of autoimmune disorders of many types. So, we're always careful screening for these through the patient's history particularly if they have developed symptoms around these life events. It is not uncommon to see a female go on birth control pills gain weight, get depressed, and then when they go off the pill and the symptoms don't change; it was the fluctuations and manipulation of hormones that may have actually triggered the autoimmune response. So, if a person has had abrupt symptom onset around puberty, pregnancy or giving birth, after going on the pill, peri-menapause, or stressful life events, check for autoimmune diseases.

Another issue with estrogens besides birth control pills and pregnancy is perimenopause. In perimenopause, females will lose their pituitary-ovarian feedback loop as a consequence of normal aging. There is a surge of estrogens created because the regulation can't be monitored well. These surges of estrogens in perimenopause can then stimulate the expression autoimmune response. Some of these dormant antigens can actually become active in menopause, and all of a sudden, these people have an immune attack against their thyroid, their joints, or other tissues, and when their immune system attacks their tissues, especially involving thyroid, they get a surge of hormones in the blood stream which then flushes their metabolic rate. They get hot flashes; they get insomnia; they get irritability. And, they blame it on a deficiency of estrogen from going through menopause but it's the immune attack that was promoted from the estrogen fluctuations through menopause, NOT an estrogen deficiency! Quite contraire, it's the estrodiol bounces and the autoimmune inflammation that is causing the symptoms; these people don't respond well to estrogens.

So, anytime you see a postmenopausal female that developed hot flashes, insomnia, and irritability but wasn't resolved with estrogens, and especially if they have a history of being hypothyroid, you have to consider over-activity of the autoimmune response. Often the hot flashes will be totally normalized by using protocols like regulatory T cell support, Th1/Th2 modulation, getting off gluten, and clearing the antigens in question.

We know that heavy metals have a great potential to become an antigen in an autoimmune disease since they are by nature an un-killable invader that is ubiquitous in our environment. The problem is we've always theorized this in alternative healthcare models, but there hasn't really been much published on this until recently. In 2006 in the Journal of Neuroendocrinology Letters a paper was published, entitled: "Removal of Dental Amalgams Decreases Anti-TPO and Anti-Thyroglobulin Autoantibodies in Patients with Autoimmune Thyroiditis." The conclusion of the paper was removal of mercury-containing dental amalgams in patients with mercury hypersensitivity may contribute to successful treatment of autoimmune thyroiditis.

Ed's story

"I've watched my wife and her mother both die of cancer in the same year, which was just two years after I sat beside her father's bed as he passed away from kidney disease prompted by his Type II Diabetes. My wife and her mother both struggled with hypothyroid, Fibromyalgia, and chronic depression before getting cancer that was diagnosed just six months apart. We went the traditional medical approach for everything even though I grew up in a very alternative healthcare family. My father was an osteopath and a naturopath who believed in natural healing whenever possible. My sister and I never went to another doctor. I really regret not being stronger in pushing alternative possibilities but Carla's family was so engrained in the medical model that they were never open to change. What I know now about autoimmune diseases and the genetic connection with gluten and casein, I think I might have been able to convince my wife that the evidence is too great to ignore. Our children will follow a different way; I'm completely convinced that I will be able help them not follow in the same footsteps thanks to this information. You've saved my children even though it's too late for my wife."

Another major autoimmune trigger that is commonly overlooked is insulin surges. Insulin is a hormone secreted by the pancreas in the presence of blood glucose. It attaches to the glucose and helps carry it into the cell to make energy. Insulin surges occur when gross fluctuations in glucose swing into the system; these surges seem to promote the autoimmune response. If a person has either insulin resistance (higher than normal blood glucose) or hypoglycemia, as they get swings in insulin and further tissue destruction. A paper that was published in the European Journal of Endocrinology in 2004, entitled, "High Prevalence of Autoimmune Thyroiditis in Patients with Polycystic Ovarian Syndrome." Polycystic ovarian syndrome is a condition when a female is producing too much insulin due to a variety of issues; this paper links PCOS with autoimmune disorders at an astounding rate.

Blood sugar issues can be categorized into insulin resistance patterns or hypoglycemia patterns. People with insulin resistance typically complain of fatigue after meals, craving sugar after meals, the desire to nap especially after eating a high amount of carbohydrates. Insulin resistant patients eat carbohydrates that quickly break down to circulating glucose, insulin surges to accompany glucose into the cell but, as they attempt to try to get across the cell membrane into the cell, the receptor sites don't work. So, the glucose goes into body fat, that's why they get so tired because the lipogenesis process takes place causing the characteristic fatigue after meal.

We'll talk more about this later but one of the things you always want to make sure with any autoimmune patient is to nutritionally support them with compounds that enhance the activity of these receptor sites.

Cindy's Story

To All of You Incredible People!!!

I have been coming to The Upper Room for over two years now, at first 4 days a week, then 3 and then 2 days. Every time, and I mean EVERY time I have been there I have been greeted and treated with such a warm and caring manner. You are all very special people and together make a great team. I am so incredibly grateful to have had my "angel" encounter with Sarah on the path that brought me to you and is without a doubt part of God's plan. My healing has been physical, emotional and spiritual and you consistently provide what I need to get better.

Dr. Conners, you are an amazing person. You have taken a risk on me and I will never forget that. I will never know for sure what has got me to this point, what supplement, whether it's the adjustment, the LBG, light beam, foot bath or just having someone join you in the belief in something that others tell you is impossible. I don't know exactly what has worked to get me to today, but I do know for a fact that I have had unconditional support from you and that has been the most important. You never promised me anything, but you also never told me it was impossible. You have provided an environment in which I could believe in a miracle without any hesitation or doubt. Thank you for supporting me to freely shoot for the stars! You know me, I will continue to expect improvement until I'm driving cars, running marathons all without the use of toxic (elephant bait) seizure medications. I would fully expect you to support me with all those dreams.

I'm looking forward to 2010. My hope is that there are a few more layers to shed. We will see what God has in store this next year.

You are not only giving my life back to me, you are giving two kids a chance to have their mother, Rob his wife, a few parents their daughter and several people a sister. You take a personal risk to treat me the way you do but in my opinion, it's worth it!

I am so grateful to have all of you on this incredible journey back to health. It takes patience, courage and strength that only God can provide and that along with your support I am going to get through this so that I provide an example of what those crazy natural healing people can do. I will proudly shout that message out to the world!

Have a great week and a very nice Thanksgiving.

Your forever-grateful patient, Cindy

Infertility

We treat infertility problems by looking as holistically at the body as possible. There may be four main classifications of issues surrounding fertility:

1. Hormonal

Our job is to locate and identify the cause of your infertility, and treat it effectively and naturally. In order to accomplish this, we use specialized lab testing to completely reveal the nature of the soil...your internal environment. It is the condition of the soil that allows bountiful crops, and the same is true of your internal environment. Any internal stressor that affects the regulation of reproduction can and will interfere with your ability to conceive and deliver. So, not only are we creating an ideal internal environment for your baby, we are ensuring your future health as a mother.

We will evaluate all **SEVEN CRITICAL HORMONAL REQUIREMENTS** of a successful pregnancy:
1. Following menstruation, a gradual rise in FSH to stimulate production of estrogen
2. The FSH release initiates a surge of estrogen.
3. The estrogen "peak" stimulates ovulation.
4. The release of an egg causes a surge of LH
5. The surge of LH initiates a gentle release of progesterone.
6. Intercourse or alternative insemination results in fertilization.
7. The progesterone release readies the uterus for implantation.

If this cycle is altered in any way...not enough estrogen, small surge of FSH, etc., etc., then there will be no pregnancy. Often infertility medications and IVF are overlooking the need for fertile soil. This is probably why this forcing of pregnancy is only effective from 30-50% of the time; and it does nothing to address the health of the Mother and baby.

2. Neurological

From a Neurological point of view, the Brain and nervous system play an integral part of the fertility process. Besides the obvious Brain connections and its firings to produce hormonal release, the Brain, particularly the Frontal Lobes and Midbrain, must function in balance to allow the pregnancy to 'hold'.

Neurological Disconnection Syndrome and its subsequent treatment with Brain Based Therapy is best described as altered firing pathways in the Brain. These pathways are like roads, and the more frequent the roads are used, it's as if they become paved for easier travel. This is what we call Neural Plasticity; the more a pathway is fired, the stronger it becomes. Neural Plasticity is a double edged sword, but we use it to our advantage when we design specific Brain Based Therapies to correct aberrant pathways. This is perhaps the most commonly missed component in treating infertility!

3. Autoimmune/Metabolic imbalance

If Neuronal Plasticity is the most commonly overlooked piece in treating infertility, then the Immune System ranks a close second. The autoimmune response is present in many infertility cases and if not corrected, the women may be destroying their own fetus.

It is important to understand that an autoimmune disorder is a 'state' that the immune system is in. It is NOT a disease of an organ; and even though it is given a multitude of names depending on the tissue currently affected, it is a STATE of the immune system attacking the tissue it was meant to protect.

Other things that are found with autoimmune processes are decreased hepatic (liver) and biliary (gallbladder and bile ducts) clearance. When we look at the detoxification processes of the body we understand there exists Phase I and Phase II pathways. Both these phases are highly nutrient dependant and the Gastro-Intestinal disturbances, decreased gut motility, and decreased absorption rates autoimmune processes decreases the ability for the patient to do the very thing they NEED to do – Detoxify!

These toxins can become Antigens that may settle anywhere along critical pathways necessary for fertilization and implantation. Where the Antigen exists is the site of greatest inflammation.

We test every patient for autoimmune disorders regardless of their past conditions!

4. Structural Interference

If a woman has ever taken exogenous hormones, including the pill or progesterone creams, has ever had any pelvic trauma, has had any inflammatory response in the pelvic area or abdomen, or has any history of PID, Endometriosis or PCOS, structure must be addressed.

These and other issues may cause adhesions near the ovaries and fallopian tubes that may physically interfere with the timing and motion of egg and sperm flow and severely affect both fertilization and implantation.

We use specific physical techniques and special tools to reduce this inflammation and detoxify the pelvic area.

Perhaps the most common cause of infertility in the United States today is polycystic ovary syndrome (PCOS). Tied to number three above, PCOS is a metabolic condition driven by metabolic disruptions of dysglycemia. Higher levels of insulin as well as estrogen/testosterone ratios literally shut down the hypothalamus-pituitary link. If this metabolic imbalance is not addressed, you are fighting a losing battle to achieve pregnancy and health.

Complicating Factors

The first obvious step in treating autoimmune diseases is to find out what the mechanism is. Asking the question, "Why?" is what we're going through in this book. But it becomes more complicated the more longstanding the disease has been because other systems of the body become affected. One seldom has solely an autoimmune attack on their thyroid; they also may have dysglycemia issues, lipid handling issues, cardio/heart issues, liver issues, adrenal issues, or pituitary issues. Commonly, an autoimmune individual has digestive issues, gallbladder problems, and kidney, prostate and hormonal issues as well. Simply, one cannot separate the systems and if something is not working right, all the dominoes begin to fall.

I want to go through some of these individually though we have to talk a little bit about your blood chemistry to do so. Most people that have autoimmune diseases have been to numerous different doctors and many times have been told that the blood work that was done was normal or there were just a few things out of normal, and those things were treated as individual conditions. And typically, especially if the person went to a traditional medical doctor, they were treated with medications simply to alter the blood test that was abnormal, and they were told that all was okay when the blood tests came back within lab ranges.

It's important to understand that there's a difference between lab range normals and functional range normals. When we talk about functional medicine, we're discussing that we see the body a little bit differently and that the ranges on lab values are much narrower. Lab range 'abnormals' are looking for what may be referred as pathological abnormalities within blood markers. What we want to see are the functional abnormalities. So if we look at the markers that examine them within functional rages, we see a lot of abnormalities and that can point to different disease processes that are taking place from a functional standpoint and how an autoimmune disease ends up progressing and attacking different organs. From both a hormonal and neurological standpoint, your body is a holistic organism that you can't separate. One cannot treat the kidney without affecting numerous other organs. Likewise, when an autoimmune disease attacks the thyroid, the pituitary, brain, heart, or gut, it's going to affect every other organ in the body in some way. Your lab markers could reveal a lot of the areas of attack that we need to address.

Let's go through some of the different blood tests that you most likely have had done, and I want to give you a better understanding of what those blood tests actually look like. First of all, I want to mention that functional blood testing can be very predictable. It' can help us balance the person's dysfunctional systems, and it should be a course of action taken by every practitioner to make sure they get as much lab work done as possible. It gives us a glimpse at the primary, secondary, and tertiary systems that we want to treat. When you're dealing with an autoimmune disease, you need to treat all of it at once. It is futile to try to correct an autoimmune disorder by trying to be systematic about treating one system at a time. Because of the interconnection and the interrelationships that are there, you have to hit it pretty hard and heavy from the start or you're not going to have a whole lot of success.

If you've done your discovery process and find out what the antigen is, let's say it is heavy metal toxicity, and you attempt to detoxify through chelation without investigating the other systems, you are destined for complications. The autoimmune process has damaged so many other systems that if you don't support and correct those at the same time, the detoxification of the heavy metal could actually make the person worse, meaning that in chelation of a heavy metal, you're going to have some of it being dropped back into the blood. If it settles in another organ system that is currently dysfunctional because of the longstanding autoimmune disease, it can greatly increase the possibility of another autoimmune attack or, worse, that organ shutting down. So, you really don't want to play with correction of an autoimmune disorder without doing a thorough assessment of the body so that you know other organ systems that you need to support at the same time.

So let's go through some of the standard blood chemistry markers that those people would get if they went into their doctor and got a blood work up. Typically, they would get glucose, cholesterol, the fats, triglycerides, LDL, HDL, iron, total iron binding capacity, ferritin, hemoglobin, hematocrit, RBCs, MCVs, MCH, MCHC, RDW, platelets, white blood cells, neutrophils, lymphocytes, monocytes, eosinophils, basophils, and then the thyroid markers of TSH and T4 are typically done. But it's important to do a more thorough thyroid assessment, and we'll talk about that in just a bit. Also, one wants alkaline phosphate, liver tests like AST, ALT, GGTP, total bilirubin, total protein breakdown into the albumin and globulin portions, the A/G ratio, sodium, potassium, chloride levels, carbon dioxide, blood, urea, nitrogen, creatinine, calcium, magnesium, phosphorus, uric acid. These are standard tests that are run on people, but I can't over-emphasize the difference between a pathological range and a functional range because that could tell us a world of a difference regarding the health of, and functional damage to other organ systems.

Dysglycemia

Blood markers can reveal functionally compromised systems; we will review a few of the more common ones in autoimmune disorders. First, let's start with glucose since it is a system that must be addressed in all autoimmune conditions. Glucose is a simple sugar that your body needs in order to create ATP. Glucose goes into the bloodstream, and then it's bound by insulin which is actually a hormone produced in the pancreas; insulin helps carry glucose across the cell membrane and each cell needs glucose in order to survive. Glucose is our major form of energy in the body because glucose, once brought across the cell membrane, is brought into the mitochondria of the cell, a little organelle that produces bundles of energy called ATP with which our body can do the functions that it needs to do. So glucose is a very important sugar that we need in our system, but it needs to be in a correct balance.

Pathological ranges of glucose tend to be 65 to 125 and, historically, anything over 125 mg/dl of glucose for a 12-hour fasting individual, the person is diagnosed with diabetes. But we tend to look at a functional range between 85 and 100; we don't want to see people over 100 nor do we want to see them under 85. Many times, people will go to their doctor and have a glucose of 75, and they're told that their blood sugar is doing great, you're not pre-diabetic, and they see that as a success. But from a functional standpoint, that person is experiencing a dysglycemic state, meaning that they're actually hypoglycemic, and they may be having symptoms that are going along with that.

It's very important to do fasting blood tests. I can't tell you how many patients I have come into our office that bring blood work with them, and my first question is always, "Did you have a 12-hour fast before you had the blood drawn?" And most of the time, they say, "no, I wasn't instructed to". It's always better to have a fast where there's no food or drink other than water before the blood is drawn.

Blood glucose, if not needed to produce immediate energy, is stored as a glycogen in the liver. The problem that we have with consumption of too many carbohydrates is that we have too much circulating glucose. When you have an overabundance of circulating glucose, your pancreas is working overtime producing insulin to bind to these glucose molecules in an attempt to break it into the cell that doesn't need it. So if a person is sedentary, their cells are not demanding glucose to produce energy because no more energy is necessary in that cell, and glucose plus insulin comes knocking at the cell door. At the cell membrane there is an enzyme called a receptor site that accepts the glucose across its wall like a doorway with a lock and key mechanism. The key is the insulin that's inserted into the receptor site, which is the lock; it unlocks the door thereby letting glucose into the cell. But when the cell doesn't need glucose, and there is an overabundance of circulating glucose from an over consumption of carbohydrates, the lock can be constantly 'stripped', you could say. And over time, where the person is consuming high amounts of carbohydrates, not exercising, and the cells do not need the excess glucose, the cell membranes and their receptor sites fail to work, or become down-regulated. This is what we call 'insulin resistance'; the receptor sites in the cell membranes become less receptive to the insulin, and to the degree that that takes place is the degree that you'll have a higher circulating glucose in the blood. And the higher circulating glucose brings us to a diagnosis of diabetes.

But, again, we're not so concerned with the diagnosis; we're concerned about the mechanism. And so, what we see from a functional standpoint of a fasting glucose over 100, we already know what mechanism is taking place. We don't wait until the glucose is over a certain point; we want to be able to treat the mechanism before it becomes a pathological condition.

Again, I just try to emphasize the difference between a pathological range and a functional range. We want to treat high glucose that's over 100 and get the person on a different diet, correct cortisol levels, and balance hormones that are going to help stimulate and normalize glucose levels before or at least during the elimination of antigens. If this is not done, the person will crash! Failure to address the big picture is the reason why we see so many patients who have been to six other doctors who attempted correction with no success. It's like trying to put a puzzle together without all the pieces

Cholesterols

Cholesterol is another test that is in the news all the time. This is really the only test in the book that the pathological range and the functional range are pretty much equal. It's funny that it is and the only reason why, is that there are statin drugs on the market that are very successful at lowering cholesterol levels. So they have lowered the pathological range so that the diagnosis may be made more readily in order to justify the prescription of the statin medication. We're not going to go into the dangers of statin medications, but I implore you to Google it for yourselves. When a patient has cholesterol of something over 200, we want to look at the reason why the cholesterol is that high and correct the cause, the faulty mechanisms that are causing the high cholesterol. We don't want to artificially lower the cholesterol by giving the person another toxin that their body has to get rid of and could theoretically become an antigen in an autoimmune condition as well.

We want to look at other markers as well and determine why the liver is overproducing cholesterol. Often, we find the person has a fatty liver condition. That's where there's fat infiltration in the liver cells and the cholesterol is being overproduced as an attempt to self-lubricate. LDL is typically considered bad cholesterol but with autoimmune conditions, it's important to note that LDL will be increased as part of the inflammatory response; it's a marker to look at that could point to an early autoimmune condition. HDL's are considered the good cholesterol, but high HDL levels can point to functional disease processes as well. It's also important to know that, as we previously discussed about insulin resistance, insulin resistance is going to decrease the HDL production as well and increase the total elevated cholesterol. Again, pointing to the fact that we don't want to look at just one marker, we have to look at all of them in conjunction, in relationship, with each other.

Anemia

The iron that we look at is also important because iron is a component of the hemoglobin group. It carries iron and transports oxygen to the body's tissue. So, we look at iron in relationship to the total iron-binding capacity or the TIBC, the ferritin levels, the transferrin levels, and the hemoglobin. The hemoglobin is really the vehicle that carries oxygen and carbon dioxide to the tissues. Cells need fuel in order to function; the main fuel that's needed by cells is glucose and oxygen. If there's a deficiency in the carrying capacity and the transport of oxygen and glucose to the cell, and a problem with the cell membrane, so that glucose and oxygen are unable to enter the cell, the person is going to have dysfunction within that system that is having that transportation problem.

As was stated previously, it's very common for people that are autoimmune to have anemias. Iron anemia is just one of those, but we can't just take a person that has low iron and put them on an iron supplement. It's very important to look at everything else in a person. Iron is a heavy metal on the periodic table, and it can be one of the greatest sources of heavy metal toxicity, from taking wrong sources of iron. Don't just look at a snapshot; take the whole movie. It's like taking a verse of the Bible out of context and creating an entire, aberrant theology; it's wrong and dangerous.

Other tests we run are red blood cells, hematocrit, the MCV or the mean corpuscular volume, the mean corpuscular hemoglobin concentration, the MCHC, the red cell size distribution width, that's the RDW. This could change in iron deficiency anemia, but can help with the differential diagnosis whether the decreased iron is due to true iron deficiency anemia, in that case, the RDW would be increased, or is the deficiency due to a degenerative disease or an autoimmune disease, in that case, the RDW might be within normal ranges, again, making a point to do all the tests.

Immune agents

The white blood cell system is assessed looking at neutrophils, lymphocytes, monocytes, eosinophils, and basophils. Remember, in autoimmune disease, we break down the lymphocytes into all their subcomponents. Again, the Th1 lymphocytes are the T cells that are the immediate-response killer cells, the cytotoxic cells that are the police force of your immune system. So they are the ones that are sent out immediately to attack the incoming invader antigen, and if they can't do their job right away, then the B cells or the Th2 system is put into action in order to create antibodies and will tag the antigen so that the Th1 system can eventually kill it. This is what we look for in autoimmune disease testing, what we described earlier as a breakdown of the Th1/Th2 markers. The cytokine testing reveals if the person is Th1 or Th2 dominant, which part of this system is hyper-firing, very important in order to be able to calm the person's symptoms down while you're getting rid of the antigen that is stimulating the Th1 or Th2 dominance in the first place.

Thyroid panels

As we look at the thyroid panels, most commonly, a patient may come in with just a TSH done, maybe a TSH and a T4, both inadequate to properly assess the thyroid gland. Commonly a person has been placed on replacement thyroid hormones simply by looking at the TSH. The TSH is a thyroid-stimulating hormone; the old name for it was thyrotropin, which is released by the pituitary. Part of the brain called the hypothalamus speaks to the pituitary through another hormone called thyrotropin-releasing hormone (TRH) and tells the pituitary to release TSH hormone. TSH hormone then goes down and communicates to the thyroid, and then, with the stimulation of the thyroid by the TSH, the thyroid releases both T3 which is the active form of the thyroid and T4 which is the inactive form which must then be converted through a process in the liver, in the gut, and some of the other organs into the active form of T3. Actually, the thyroid makes T4 to T3 at about a ratio of 93% to 7%. So the thyroid is only releasing the 7% of the active form of the thyroid hormone; some have speculated that this may be due to the fact that the thyroid's job is to produce a majority of the inactive form so when needed, the liver could convert it into the active form. There could be other thyroid problems present in this chain of events like thyroid hormone 'underconversion'. This is the inability of T4 to convert to T3 in the liver, gut, or other organs causing a decreased active thyroid hormone and hypothyroid symptoms, really not a thyroid problem whatsoever. That's why it's important to do all the testing of the thyroid so you could really get a good idea of what is causing the thyroid dysfunction.

But like we said before, most commonly, the problem is really not a thyroid problem whatsoever; it's an autoimmune problem that's attacked the thyroid. So, in a sense, it's something outside of the thyroid that needs to be treated, but the attack is on the thyroid cells themselves, causing the decreased production of T4 and T3.

So in review, an autoimmune disease may leave a person Th1 dominant, the part of the immune system that is the police force, not the part that makes antibodies. If that is the case, then they won't readily show antibodies against their tissue even though the body has destroyed that tissue through that autoimmune response. Therefore don't rely on thyroid antibody testing to reveal an autoimmune attack on the thyroid! If the person is Th2 dominant, then it's easy to see the antibodies for that tissue, and they'll readily show up positive, an easy diagnosis. But that's why we want to get the interleukin tests, the other cytokine tests, so we can see the balance of whether they're firing a Th1 response or a Th2 response with the autoimmune disease.

Liver/GI tests

The typical liver tests that are run are AST and ALT previously called SGOT and SGPT, respectively. These are enzymes that are present in tissues that have a very high metabolic activity such as the liver, the heart, skeletal muscle, and the brain. These markers are released after that tissue has normal cell death, giving us a functional range for AST and ALT. When they are high, there may be an abnormally high amount of cell death or injury to the organ, and we want to investigate it a little further.

ALT is also an enzyme in high concentrations in the liver; therefore, it's considered a liver function test. If there's damage to the liver from an exogenous source, the AST and the ALT will rise. We have to remember that, very commonly, since the liver is one of our major organs of detoxification, any stress on the liver due to necessary detoxification can raise these two enzyme levels. Unfortunately, one of the most common reasons we see a rise in liver enzymes is where the patient is detoxifying a prescription medication that they're on.

Bilirubin should be separated into indirect and direct. It's a measurement of breakdown of red blood cells; total protein should also be separated into albumin and globulin levels. The albumin acts to regulate the movement of water between the tissues and the bloodstream, very important as far as the body being able to detoxify cellular debris and waste products. Globulin is a group of different fats broken down into alpha, beta, and gamma globulins. The ratio between albumin and globulin (called the A/G ratio) is a marker that when decreased, may indicate the beginning of liver dysfunction, a dysfunction in the stomach cells, or a decreased production of hydrochloric acid, and a disruption in digestion.

While we can't discuss dysglycemia without discussing a blood test known as hemoglobin A1c, the best blood test to help diagnose diabetic states. The functional range of hemoglobin A1C is, of course, tighter than the pathological range. We look for it to be not greater than 5.7. It is truly measuring the amount of glucose in the blood that is tied to the glyconated hemoglobin. So, 90% of the hemoglobin in your blood is hemoglobin A and that stands for the adult type or mature type of hemoglobin. One of these components is hemoglobin A1C, and it is the glucose-bound hemoglobin. It's really the most accurate measurement of insulin resistance because it's not as sensitive to daily fluctuations. Whether you ate some ice cream today and didn't eat it the next day, and therefore, my glucose levels changed over the course of the day, it's not a test that is, at least at this point, a test that can be measured at home with a home measuring device like glucose is; therefore, glucose is easier to monitor on a regular basis for a patient with insulin resistance or diabetes. Hemoglobin A1C is really the appropriate test to make a diagnosis as far as how you're going to treat the patient.

Jim's Story

"I've been diabetic for about 12 years and have pretty much controlled it with diet and Metformin medication that my doctor prescribed. My health had been getting worse since I retired. My hands and wrists have bad arthritis and I think that my knees are pretty shot. Before I was told that this was part of an autoimmune disease, I was taking about 6-9 Advil each day and at least 2 Aleve for the joint pain. My shoulders, all the way down to my fingers, were so stiff in the morning I had to soak them in hot and cold water alternating just to get some motion in my wrists. I never heard of autoimmune disease but I was willing to trust the idea since nothing else was working. After 3 months of detoxifying and changing my diet (even though I'm not perfect), I can safely say that I'm getting my life back."

When dysglycemia is present with autoimmune patients, we need to help regulate it. And again, I can't overemphasize that you have to do this at the same time that you're clearing the antigens and balancing the immune system or you're going to be disappointed in your results. The way we regulate glucose is not through medication. Medication will artificially decrease the glucose levels, cause disruption in our ability to detoxify other antigens, and just create another antigen that the liver has to deal with. We compromise the detoxification pathways of the liver with the more medications we use to try to balance the patient. In our office, we like to use nutraceuticals, herbal formulas, diet and exercise that have been proven to help balance the dysglycemic state. If the patient will not comply with the diet, we don't even accept them as a patient; it's important to be serious about this. And as much as I understand that addictive states with food are extremely common, it's really a life or death situation with this individual.

When we speak of the gastrointestinal system, we're speaking of everything from the type of food you choose, you chewing your food, your ability to make saliva, the ability of your stomach cells to make hydrochloric acid and your intestines to secrete the necessary enzymes, the bile that's made in the liver that's going to breakdown your fats, and the intestines to move the food through the gut, and the intestinal villi to be free enough to absorb the nutrients, the capillary bed in the intestinal wall to be healthy enough to absorb the nutrients, the large intestine to absorb water and to create the feces that will be ultimately deposited in the toilet in a timely fashion so that we don't reabsorb all the toxins that our body is trying to get rid of. If that isn't a run-on sentence, I don't know what is.

The most common gastrointestinal disorder is a condition of decreased stomach acid production called hypochlorhydria. Most gastric reflux issues and symptoms of hyperacidemia causing most people to reach for Tums, Rolaids, or Prilosec are really problems of a decreased hydrochloric acid production. That seems silly to someone who has these stomach issues with increased acid and burping up acid. They will tell you that, "You must be crazy. I don't have decreased hydrochloric acid production. I must have an increased hydrochloric acid production because I'm burping up acid into my gut and my doctor is telling me it's damaging the lower part of my esophagus. Therefore, I need to get on a medication that's going to be a proton-pump inhibitor and block the acid production of my stomach cells." Well, this is completely counterproductive if you understand the mechanism and it's just downright malpractice for doctors to continue to prescribe this type of medication because it's leading to malabsorption, maldigestion, inability to use proteins, and all sorts of problems for the patient. This is just an absolute vicious cycle that you have to break, and it's difficult for patients that have been on these medications for years for their body to go through some changes to get their hydrochloric acid stomach levels back to normal.

Your stomach is the only place in your body that needs to be highly acidic. A pH of 1.0 is really much needed in your stomach and any imbalances that are going to cause maldigestion. Hydrochloric acid helps with the breakdown of fats and carbohydrates, and it's your primary digestive factor for protein. So, when proteins go into the stomach, hydrochloric acid needs to be there to break that protein down. When a person has a diet high in additives, colorings, flavorings, and toxins that block the beta cells of the stomach to secrete hydrochloric acid, the cycle begins. This leads to a decrease in the hydrochloric acid and a decrease mucus formation, which is a precursor to H. pylori infections and stomach ulcer formation.

But primarily, a decreased HCl production will lead to a decreased digestion of proteins. When you have a bolus of food that's improperly digested not entering into the small intestine in a timely factor, it sits in the stomach and pushes the little acid that is there up through the cardiac sphincter into the esophagus; you get reflux that irritates the diaphragm and the lower esophagus. While antacids will take the pain away, they perpetuate the negative cycle. What the patient needs to do is heal the stomach lining and the stomach cells so they can start producing the right amount of hydrochloric acid, so the protein can get digested, so the bolus could move through the stomach and into the small intestine and get properly digested and absorbed. The reflux will stop when the mechanism is corrected.

If we're just going to treat the symptoms, not only are we not helping the patient, we're actually propagating the disease process itself, and we're creating a sicker patient in the end. Antacids create a state where the stomach is more alkaline, destroying our first line of defense against opportunistic organisms. Virus, bacteria, parasites, molds, fungus, and living biological toxins that we consume and are exposed to on a daily basis are not supposed to live beyond the normal acid slurry in the stomach.

There are numerous tests to assess the gastrointestinal system, typically, a traditional medical doctor will do some sort of scope in order to look for gross damage in the intestinal wall; they look to see if a person has any ulceration, damage, or tumor growth, and of course, that's necessary to rule out. Testing for parasites and H. pylori infections is a must. Digestive blood markers include triglycerides, lipid panels with cholesterol, HDL, LDL testing.

When we work on clearing the digestive system out, there's traditionally an alternative health care model called the 4-R program. The 4-R program stands for removing toxins, re-inoculation of the gut, replacing missing nutrients and good symbiotic bacteria in the gut, and repairing any damage to the gut, so it can properly function.

So removing includes destroying any parasitology, bacteria, and yeast overgrowths. Treating some of these conditions may need drug intervention, that's where traditional medicine works very well in dealing with quick-kill measures for these bowel toxins. However, a person can use different nutrients and an herbal approach as well. It tends to be very effective in dealing with these things without side effects of the medication.

The re-inoculation phase involves replenishing the GI tract with the symbiotic bacteria such as Lactobacillus acidophilus, and bifidobacterium. It also includes adding digestive enzymes and hydrochloric acid. Sometimes, a person needs to be on these things for a very long time, even for life, especially if there has been severe damage to the gut wall and the stomach cells. Typically, it takes anywhere between 6-12 months before the stomach can balance out its own HCl production and start dealing with breaking down protein on its own.

The repair phase includes proper nutritional support to heal the gastrointestinal mucosal lining. In repairing the mucosal lining, we used different supplements and herbals that have history and research behind it that will help mucus production in the gut so that it can hold the good bacteria. Malabsorption is often from damage to the mucosal lining that needs to be healed.

Adrenal Stress

Adrenal insufficiency and adrenal stress is measured through the Adrenal Stress Index. The adrenal glands are two glands that are embryologically neurological tissue that sit right above each kidney. They are very important in function of hormonal activity, energy and stress management. The adrenal glands are made up of an exterior covering or cortex of the gland which produces steroid hormones cortisol, aldosterone, progesterone, and DHEA. And then, the inner part of the adrenal gland is called the medulla that produces the catecholamines such as epinephrine and norepinephrine which have to do with your sympathetic nervous system function.

Our nervous system is made up of two basic components, a voluntary nervous system and an involuntary nervous system. The involuntary nervous system (the autonomic nervous system or one might say an automatic nervous system) is made up of two separate components that work in harmony and balance. They are the sympathetic part of the autonomic nervous system and the parasympathetic part. The sympathetic part may be best termed as the fight, flight, or freeze mechanism; the parasympathetic part has to do our metabolism, digestion, and the calming aspect of the autonomic nervous system. Both need to be in balance. If a person is hyper-sympathetic or is functioning in a very high stress situation for extended periods of time their adrenal glands are in a state of hyperfunction and can end up burning out. We weren't meant to live in a society where we're constantly running away from a grisly bear.

Burning the candle at both ends tends to cause a high degree of hyper-sympathetic nervous system function, which relates to greater adrenal output and adrenal stress. Prolonged stress leads to adrenal fatigue and exhaustion, not to mention exhaustion to the other parts of the brain that are the stimulators of the adrenal and the pituitary output. A lifestyle issue may have been an initiator for this, but adrenal fatigue is a negative cycle that will drive the autoimmune patient into the ground if not concurrently addressed.

Lisa's Story

"Bill and I have been married for fourteen years since I was 22 years old. I had just graduated for college and even though Bill was ready for a family right away, I wanted to wait a few years to make some money and get some of my student loans paid. When I turned 28, I thought I'd better listen to my mother regarding my 'biological clock'. I was ready to start a family so I got off the pill. After a year of trying and nothing was happening, we made an appointment with my regular doctor. He did a bunch of tests on both Bill and I and I only remember him saying that there was no reason that I couldn't get pregnant, so we just kept trying. Another year passed and we were both starting to get a little worried. My doctor referred me to a fertility specialist and we went through a lot of expensive testing to be offered even more expensive procedures that had no guarantee. A friend referred me to her doctor, a chiropractic neurologist who specialized in autoimmune diseases and fertility problems. I thought, "you're *kidding right?' I could not, for the life of me, think that he was going to be able to do anything for me! Well, I gave it a shot, he offered a 100% guaranteed plan and Bill said we had nothing to lose. Bill was wrong; I lost my infertility! I was pregnant in 6 months and have a beautiful baby girl. It turned out that I had Hashimoto's disease, which is an autoimmune problem with the thyroid. That is why I couldn't get pregnant. None of my other doctors caught it."*

The adrenal cortex also makes some of our sex hormones and a very important percentage of them in the postmenopausal female. The ability of the adrenal glands to secrete these reproductive hormones postmenopausal has a very important impact on the intensity of menopausal symptoms. If a woman is going through hot flashes and sweating, anger issues, and an inability to handle stress, it has to do with the fluctuations of estrogen from a fatigued adrenal system. The adrenal glands are suppose to regulate the estrodiol levels in the blood as the ovaries are down-regulated with age, giving the woman a smooth, symptom-less transaction into menopause.

When a woman becomes perimenopausal, the pituitary is decreasing its production of follicle-stimulating hormone, the hormone that functions in release of estradiol. The adrenals take over at this point to balance the decreased production. If the adrenals are exhausted, they don't make up that balance in estradiol and the women has strict, strong fluctuations in estradiol levels, and end up with huge swings in energy, hot flashes, sweating, etc., that go with perimenopausal symptoms.

Cortisol is the primary glucocorticoid secreted by the adrenal cortex and increases the blood glucose concentration. A person in a high-stress situation will release more cortisol, and that cortisol increases the blood glucose. This makes a lot of sense from a sympathetic, fight or flight mechanism; when a giant grisly bear jumps on our path, we need a lot of glucose in our bloodstream for muscle cells to make ATP, so we can run away from our predator. But it doesn't make a lot of sense when our job is just extremely stressful causing our adrenals to put out vast amounts of cortisol on a daily basis. Our sympathetic nervous system can't tell the difference between a real grisly bear encounter and stock market crash; the results will be the same. The real or perceived exogenous stress source causing a hyper-adrenal output causes a hyper-cortisolemia leading to a hyper-glucose reaction and a hyper-insulinemia. This is what we call a negative cycle; it spins us downward towards greater sickness and death.

High adrenal output causes a lot of damage to other tissues and may, in itself, be a source for an autoimmune response. It certainly is a component in the autoimmune system and, again, an absolute must in treating concurrently with an autoimmune disease. Treatment is aimed at supporting the organ with chemicals called adaptogens, herbal formulas that are known to balance high and low adrenal outputs. We also use a compound called phosphatidylserine, which has a balancing affect on the hippocampal formation, the part of the brain that senses these stressful situations. It's this hippocampal-hypothalamus-pituitary-adrenal link that we want to calm down.

Common signs and symptoms of adrenal problems are going to be fatigue, headaches, and multiple allergies. Because a person's stress response is constantly firing, it fatigues their immune system. Stomach ulcers are also common as is cravings for sweets or caffeine. They'll have addictions to food, alcohol, drugs, or cigarettes. Other signs and symptoms can be dizziness, asthma issues, varicose veins, blood disorders, and blood pressure issues.

Adrenal dysfunction is also tied to the midbrain and the frontal lobes which can lead to anxiety and depression which may be the chief symptom that brings the patient to the office. We see a high number of patients today that are on brain-altering, mind-changing medication due to stress issues that are really adrenal issues affecting the frontal lobes; all these could be addressed from a functional medicine perspective, if you address all the systems that are tied together. By the time the person has symptoms that bring them into a doctor's office, whether it's a medical doctor or an alternative practitioner, there has been down regulation of multiple systems.

Though it's impossible to discuss every system and the cellular response necessary to thoroughly analyze a patient with autoimmune disease in this book, we would be amiss if we didn't discuss the gastrointestinal component because it always exists in autoimmune disorders and is essential for us getting the nutrients in order to regulate all the systems.

Other Named Autoimmune Diseases:

Amyotrophic lateral sclerosis (ALS)

Many autoimmune processes are fatal. ALS, also named Lou Gehrig's disease after the famous Baseball player who died due to ALS, is a progressive, fatal neurological disease that attacks the nerve cells (neurons) responsible for controlling muscles. In ALS, both the brain and the spinal neurons degenerate and die. ALS is triggered by diverse antigens; some are toxic exposures, injuries and infections. One study in Guam looked at the pathogeneses of the disease revealed high aluminum in the water and a plant excitatory neurotoxin as possible causes. In Italy, an increasing number of soccer players have developed ALS; some have connected this with the use of illegal toxic substances or exposure to pesticides used on playing fields.

Symptoms of ALS include muscle weakening, muscles waste away and twitch. Patients with ALS lose their strength and the ability to move their arms, legs, and body. Muscles in the diaphragm and chest wall fail, and then patients lose the ability to breathe. In most cases the disease does not impair a person's mind, a small percentage of patients may experience problems with memory or decision-making, and there is growing evidence that some may even develop dementia.

Bell's palsy

Bells Palsy is a sudden onset of inflammation in the Facial Nerve (Cranial Nerve 7). This is often temporary but left untreated, can become permanent. Most noticed as a facial droop caused by inflammation and paralysis of the facial nerve. The inflammation in the facial nerve is the result of autoimmune processes and can involve the either side. A swollen facial nerve can be compressed in the facial canal. Facial palsy can be an early manifestation of Lymes disease.

Usually the causative factor is thought to be herpes virus, cytomegalovirus (CMV) or Borrelia by most standard medical professionals, but any antigen can be at cause. Facial palsy may be triggered by exposure to cold air draft, high amounts of stress and everything else that may fire an immune response.

Symptoms range in severity from mild weakness causing a facial droop to total uni-lateral paralysis and may include twitching, weakness, drooping eyelid or corner of the mouth, drooling, dry eyes, impairment of taste, and excessive tearing in the eye. Bell's palsy can occur on both sides when accompanied by Guillian Barre syndrome.

Cardiovascular Autoimmune Diseases

Some speculate that the leading cause of death in the world, heart disease, is due to inflammatory reactions in the capillary wall at the site of atherosclerosis. It is the plaguing, caused by a high homocysteine level which then etches the arterial wall. This 'scratch' is then healed with a cholesterol patch. The high homocysteine levels are tied to inability to absorb vitamin B12 and folic acid – a problem endemic in autoimmune disorders. These nutrients are essential in converting homocysteine to its harmless substrate. Some have termed this celiac disease myocarditis, which is a misnomer since celiac disease accompanies few of the coronary conditions. It can be ANY autoimmune disorder that can lead to cardiovascular autoimmune disease. However it is a treatable condition and anti-gliadin and other antibodies as well as cytokines can be checked in patients who are unresponsive to conventional treatments. These patents respond to dietary management and TH1/TH2 control, antigen removal, sublingual B12/Folic Acid supplementation, and diet guidelines that are in the Gluten Diet section.

Chronic Inflammatory Demyelinating Polyneuropathy (CIDP)

CIDP is an acquired immune-mediated inflammatory disorder of the peripheral nervous system. The disorder is sometimes called chronic relapsing polyneuropathy. CIDP is closely related to Guillain-Barré syndrome and it is considered the chronic counterpart of that acute disease. Its symptoms are also similar to progressive inflammatory neuropathy. An asymmetrical variant of CIDP is known as Lewis-Sumner syndrome.

The pathologic hallmark of the disease is loss of the myelin sheath (the fatty covering that protects nerve fibers) of the peripheral nerves. Chronic inflammatory demyelinating polyneuropathy is believed to be due to an autoimmune response from a foreign infection attacking the peripheral nerves. As a result, the affected nerves fail to respond, or respond only weakly, to stimuli causing numbing, tingling, pain, progressive muscle weakness, loss of deep tendon reflexes, fatigue, and abnormal sensations. The likelihood of progression of the disease is high.

Dermatitis, Autoimmune Atopic or Eczema

Atopic dermatitis (AD) is a chronic, itching, inflammatory skin disease which is associated with asthma or hay fever and a familial occurrence of these conditions. The disease comes in attacks that seem to get better then worse in cycles. There are a number of different eczemas – rashes which cause the skin to become inflamed and itchy. AD is also called 'atopic eczema' or 'infantile eczema'. It affects people with dry and rough skin and may be caused by a variety of antigens.

Patients with atopic dermatitis often have elevated serum IgE levels and a hyper-sensitization to a variety of environmental allergens quite possibly due to an autoimmune response elsewhere in the body. This 'remote' autoimmune response leaves the patient hyper-Th1 or hyper-Th2, making them hyper-sensitive to a variety of allergens they would not normally react to.

Guillain–Barré syndrome (GBS)

GBS is an *acute inflammatory demyelinating polyneuropathy* (AIDP), an autoimmune disorder affecting the peripheral nervous system, usually triggered by an acute infectious process. The syndrome was named after the French physicians Guillain, Barré and Strohl, who were the first to describe it in 1916. It is sometimes called Landry's paralysis, after the French physician who first described a variant of it in 1859. It is included in the wider group of peripheral neuropathies. It is frequently severe and usually exhibits as an ascending paralysis noted by weakness in the legs that spreads to the upper limbs and the face along with complete loss of deep tendon reflexes.

The disorder is characterized by symmetrical weakness which usually affects the lower limbs first, and rapidly progresses in an ascending fashion. Patients generally notice weakness in their legs, manifesting as "rubbery legs" or legs that tend to buckle, with or without dysesthesias (numbness or tingling). As the weakness progresses upward, usually over periods of hours to days, the arms and facial muscles also become affected. Frequently, the lower cranial nerves may be affected, oropharyngeal dysphagia (drooling, or difficulty swallowing and/or maintaining an open airway) and respiratory difficulties.

Guillain–Barré syndrome is due to an immune response on the peripheral nerves and damage to the myelin, the fatty insulating layer of the nerve, leading to a muscle paralysis that may be accompanied by sensory or autonomic disturbances.

Lymes disease

Lymes disease was first recognized in 1975 after a number of cases occurred in the same town in North America. It subsequently took its name from this town, which was called Old Lymes, in Connecticut. Lymes disease which is spread to humans by a small bug called the deer tick. This bug passes a spirochete called Treponema Pallidum to the human. Lymes borreliosis is due to infection with the spirochete Borrelia burgdorferi, and is associated with persistent infection unless treated with antibiotics within the first several weeks. The persistent nature of infection by B. burgdorferi can lead to development of chronic autoimmune disease. Lymes transforms into multiple autoimmune conditions.

Klempner did a study in chronic Lymes and found that antibiotics did not change the course of disease once it became chronic. Then NIH (National Institutes of Health) recommended that autoimmune basis of Lymes disease needs to be explored. Currently Borrelia antibodies have been associated with remitting relapsing Multiple sclerosis, Thyroiditis, carotid artery disease, epilepsy and arthritis.

Usually the first sign of Lymes infection is a circular 'bulls-eye' skin rash at the point of entry. This can easily be overlooked and missed if the bite is in the scalp. This follows with symptoms of tiredness, headache, joint pains, and flu-like symptoms. If not treated these symptoms may last for weeks, months, years and even decades. As the disease progresses then shortness of breath, chest pains, weakness, and tingling numbness in the legs and arms starts. Some may start to notice memory problems, difficulty concentrating and fatigue as well as joint swelling and arthritis. Usually the blood tests for Lymes show false negatives after the first 30-60 days. As with all autoimmune diseases, the first course of action is to locate and eliminate the antigen.

Migraine autoimmune headaches

Migraine affects 35 million Americans, most of whom are women. Migraine is preceded or accompanied by a sensory warning signs called a (aura), such as flashes of light, blind spots, smell or tingling in your arm or leg. A migraine headache can follow with signs and symptoms, such as nausea, vomiting and sensitivity to light and sound. Migraine pain is usually throbbing and can last for hours or even days.

Inflammatory markers go up rapidly in an attack of Migraines, CRP is elevated, the spinal fluid protein becomes elevated and more white cells are seen in the spinal fluid during a migraine attack. Migraine and epileptic seizure disorders are interrelated and like other autoimmune diseases migraines happen more in women. There may be associated epilepsy with migraine.

Migraine often comes in remissions and relapses just like autoimmune disease. Migraine is associated with women just like autoimmune disorders. Some women with Lupus present with migraine, as their first symptom. Following anti-inflammatory treatment their migraine attacks usually resolve. Many patients with lupus present with migraines secondary to severe vasospasm. These patients have anti-phospholipids antibodies and at times the migraine will only respond to steroids or cyclophosphamide. MRI scans obtained during a migraine have shown dramatic thickening of brain folds called (gyral) with enhancement which suggests inflammation.

General symptoms of Migraine

- One-sided throbbing head pain which worsens with physical movement.
- Nausea, Vomiting
- Twisted shining lines in front of the eye sometimes without a headache.
- Weakness or numbness in a hand or leg
- Sensitivity to light (Photosensitive headaches respond to magnesium)
- Sensitivity to sound, smell, and light, (patients prefers a dark room)

Multiple Sclerosis

Multiple sclerosis (MS) is a chronic, autoimmune disease in which the immune system attacks the Myelin covering the nerves in the brain and spinal cord. This is similar to CIDP neuropathy where the attack is against peripheral myelin. The myelin in the Brain and spinal cord is made by cells called oligodendrocytes and in the peripheral nerves by Schwann cells.

Multiple sclerosis can develop after exposure to Epstein-Barr virus (EBV), Chlamydia, STD's, other parasitic infestations, as well as environmental toxins and foods. The body then incorrectly directs antibodies and white blood cells against the myelin sheath, which surrounds nerves in the brain and spinal cord. This causes inflammation and injury to the myelin-sheath. This damage results in multiple areas of scarring (sclerosis). Eventually, this damage can slow or block the nerve signals that control muscle coordination, strength, sensation and vision. This damage can be visualized by a M.R.I. scan as multiple white spots in the brain.

Different Types of MS:
- **Relapsing remitting** type of MS is seen in 90% of the cases characterized by relapses (disease flare-ups), followed by periods of remission. This is the most common type. I have seen many cases where the patient was labeled as progressive MS only to find they had clear history of remissions and relapses.
- **Primary progressive** form of MS, which shows a gradual decline, without periods of remission. People with this form of MS are usually older than 40 when symptoms begin.
- **Secondary progressive.** About half the people with relapsing remitting MS eventually enter a stage of continuous deterioration referred to as secondary progressive MS.
- **Progressive M.S.** Not a good medical prognosis as the disease progresses rapidly.

Symptoms include:
- Numbness or weakness which typically occurs on one side of the body.
- Double vision, blurring of vision or sudden loss of vision (optic neuritis).
- Tingling numbness or pain one half of the body.
- Electric-shock sensations that occur with certain head movements

- Tremor, lack of coordination or unsteady gait and weakness.
- Fatigue specially after exposure to heat, or exercise.
- Dizziness or feeling of spinning.

Myasthenia Gravis

Myasthenia Gravis is a chronic autoimmune, neuromuscular disease characterized by weakness of the voluntary (skeletal) muscles of the body. The name myasthenia gravis, means "grave muscle weakness." The hallmark of myasthenia gravis is muscle weakness that increases during activity and improves after of rest.

Certain muscles such as those that control eye and eyelid movement, facial expression, chewing, talking, and swallowing are often, involved in the disorder. The muscles that control breathing, neck movements and limb movements may also be affected when a nerve impulse travels down the nerve; a chemical neurotransmitter called acetylcholine is released in the nerve ending and travels to acetylcholine (Ach) receptors located on the muscle side of the synapse, causing the muscle to contract. Among people with myasthenia gravis, this normal impulse transmission of Ach is disrupted by autoantibodies that target the body's own Ach- receptors and block them. If enough receptors are blocked by autoantibodies, then the muscle contraction will be weak, causing the symptoms of myasthenia gravis.

Many pesticides contain organophosphorus chemicals that can inhibit the acetyl cholinesterase enzyme and make myasthenia worse. Halides (like **chlorine** and **fluorine**) may pose additional risk for myasthenia gravis patients. In one case report, a patient was exposed to chlorine gas and subsequently developed generalized myasthenia gravis). Fluoride is also implicated, and fluoridated water may trigger a myasthenia gravis crisis or contribute to long-term deterioration, with extreme exhaustion and muscle weakness, so please avoid fluoride containing toothpaste.

Reflex sympathetic dystrophy R.S.D or Complex regional pain syndrome:

Complex regional pain syndrome or RSD is essentially inflammation of the autonomic nerves in a localized area. RSD has been associated with injury dating back to the Civil War. We have already described the association of autoimmune disorders with injury. In general, patients who have complex regional pain syndrome suffer from pain, sensory changes, edema, sweating, and temperature disturbance in the afflicted extremity. Chronic changes can involve the skin, nails, and bone. Persistent inflammation, of the sympathetic nervous system and the central nervous system causes this condition.

Symptoms include increased sweating, skin color changes, skin temperature changes, weakness of the affected area, swelling, as well as symptoms outside the affected dermatome.

Restless Leg Syndrome

People with restless leg syndrome, or RLS, have a creepy-crawly feeling in their legs. This causes an irresistible urge to move the legs. It's a major cause of sleep loss, as the symptoms are most likely to occur at night. It has been found that brain cells need iron, oxygen carried by hemoglobin, and activation. They get nutrients from transport molecules that carry iron from the blood. Normal brain cells have doorways that let these transport molecules into the cell. Patients with restless leg syndrome lacked these portals, known as transferrin receptors. This means in spite of adequate amounts of iron in the blood not enough of it can enter the brain to prevent molecular damage.

Previous studies have shown that bacterial overgrowth in the small intestine causes inflammatory cells to increase production of IL-6. This cytokine, in turn, is known to boost levels of hepcidin, a protein that decreases iron absorption and transport. Bacterial overgrowth in the gut could be causing the problems and natural, anti-parasitic therapy targeting the stomach and small intestine might be the solution. RLS behaves differently from other autoimmune diseases, as this condition will increase during pregnancy. RLS is seen commonly, in patients with Fibromyalgia and Irritable Bowel syndrome.

Rheumatic Autoimmune Disorders

Rheumatoid arthritis is triggered by Mycoplasma. RA is two to three times more common in women than in men and generally strikes between the ages of 20 and 50. Rheumatoid arthritis can also affect children. The diagnosis is based upon clinical examination and elevated ESR or CRP along with x-rays showing early damage in the joints.

Investigators have shown that Mycoplasma which is a small bug without a cell wall causes arthritis in humans. Mycoplasma antigens have been found in all grains and their products, they are ubiquitous in our storehouses and impossible to avoid.

In 1949 at the International Congress on Rheumatic Diseases reported the relationship between Mycoplasma and joint disease. National Institutes of Health (NIH) issued a research grants in 1950, to Thomas Brown, M.D., who reported an immunologic reaction of antigen and antibody (with Mycoplasma as the suspected antigen) as the cause of rheumatoid disease. Further support of Mycoplasma as a causative agent and antigen was proven in 1964, when a high incidence of Mycoplasma antibodies in the blood of rheumatoid arthritis patients and lupus patients was found. Also recognized was a 4:1 higher incidence of Mycoplasma antibodies in females suggesting a correlation with the higher incidences of rheumatoid arthritis in females. In1989, NIH requested grant applications for the controlled clinical trials of tetracycline therapy for rheumatoid arthritis. The preliminary results of the clinical trials, known as MIRA or Minocycline in Rheumatoid Arthritis, were promising and the NIH requested grant applications for studies of Mycoplasma as causes for rheumatoid diseases in 1993 and for a study for intravenous antibiotics for rheumatoid arthritis in 1994. The result of the MIRA clinical trial stated, that Patients who suffer from mild to moderate can benefit from Minocycline. A review of ten randomized controlled trials involving 535 patients were reviewed, reviewers reported Minocycline was associated with a clinically improvement in disease activity in RA with no absolute increased risk of side effects.

Symptoms of RA:
- Pain and swelling in joints, especially in the smaller joints of your hands and feet
- Generalized aching or stiffness in joints after sleep or after periods of rest
- Reduced motion of the affected joints; deformity of joints over time
- Weakness in muscles attached to the affected joints
- Fatigue, which can be severe during a flare-up , Low-grade fever
- General sense of not feeling well (malaise)

In RA, the joints in the wrists, hands, feet and knees are most often affected. Later in the disease, shoulders, elbows, hips, jaw and neck can be involved. It generally affects both sides of your body at the same time. Small lumps, called rheumatoid nodules, may form under the skin at pressure points and can occur at elbows, hands, feet and Achilles tendons.

Rosacea

Rosacea is a common autoimmune allergic condition characterized by symptoms of facial flushing and a spectrum of clinical signs, including erythema, telangiectasia, and coarseness of skin, edema, papules, pustules, ocular lesions and an inflammatory papulopustular eruption resembling acne. Rosacea affects mostly adults, usually people with fair skin, between the ages of 30 and 60. About 16 million Americans have this skin condition. Although it's more common in women, men may develop the disorder. Left untreated, rosacea tends to be progressive, which means it gets worse over time. Rosacea is remitting and relapsing, it flares up for a period of weeks to months and then signs & symptoms lessen for a while before rosacea flares up again.

Rosacea fulminans is a sub type of rosacea, occurs exclusively in women well past adolescence.

There is a high prevalence of Helicobacter pylori (Hp) infection seen in patients with rosacea, with evidence of dermatological improvement in patients treated with antibiotics for this infection. In a study done on Rosacea patients after eradication of Hp, 51 out of 53 treated rosacea patients became Hp negative. The symptoms of rosacea disappeared in 51 patients, markedly declined in one and remained unchanged in one patient. Conclusion from this study is that Hp eradication helps a majority of patients with Rosacea.

Scleroderma & C.R.E.S.T

Scleroderma is an autoimmune disease that can cause thickening, hardening, or tightening of the skin, blood vessels and internal organs. Scleroderma is chronic, which means it can last a long time. This is one disease in which the patients never gain weight, due to the effect it has on tightening their skin they all look skinny. They also have very hard hands, with skin around the fingers tight. They have difficulty swallowing as the esophagus is tight, so is the stomach wall tight and they cannot tolerate large meals. There are two types of scleroderma localized and systemic.

A) Systemic Scleroderma (SS) also called systemic sclerosis, the immune system causes inflammation in the small blood vessels and the collagen-producing cells located in the skin and throughout the body. SS causes the small blood vessels in the fingers to be inflamed; this causes injuries on the hands and fingers to heal slowly. In severe cases, ulcers form on the hands and fingers. People with Systemic Scleroderma are usually cold-sensitive. The inflamed small blood vessels and the reduced blood supply cause cold temperature sensitivity. Systemic Scleroderma patients also have problems with their heart, lungs and gastrointestinal tract. These problems occur as tissue builds up in the skin and organs due to inflammation.

B) Localized Scleroderma called Morphea affects the collagen-producing cells in just some areas of the body, and usually does not affect the internal organs and blood vessels. Localized Scleroderma can be seen as patches of thick skin or as a line of thick skin. The line may extend down a leg or arm.

C) A sub type of scleroderma is called CREST which has a distinct set of characteristics that give the syndrome its acronymic name. These characteristics include:

- Calcinosis: Tiny calcium deposits form under your skin, on elbows, knees and fingers; and can occur almost anywhere, in the body.
- Raynaud's phenomenon: The hands and forearms become cold and blue due to inflammation in the blood vessels the upper extremity.
- Esophageal dysfunction: Inflammation in the stomach and esophagus can cause swallowing problems and retention of fluids in the stomach.
- Sclerodactyly: Thick hard patches of skin start to calcify. This bone-like skin can even be seen on X-ray.
- Telangiectasia: Small, spider-like blood vessels start to form on lips and fingers.

Transverse Myelitis

The National Institutes of Health list Transverse myelitis as a neurological disorder caused by inflammation across both sides of one level, or segment, of the spinal cord. The term *myelitis* refers to inflammation of the spinal cord; *transverse* simply describes the position of the inflammation, that is, across the width of the spinal cord. Attacks of inflammation can damage or destroy myelin, the fatty insulating substance that covers nerve cell fibers, much like that in MS. This damage causes nervous system scars that interrupt communications between the nerves in the spinal cord and the rest of the body.

Symptoms of transverse myelitis include a loss of spinal cord function over several hours to several weeks. What usually begins as a sudden onset of lower back pain, muscle weakness, or abnormal sensations in the toes and feet can rapidly progress to more severe symptoms, including paralysis, urinary retention, and loss of bowel control. Although some patients recover from transverse myelitis with minor or no residual problems, others suffer permanent impairments that affect their ability to perform ordinary tasks of daily living.

Autoimmune in nature, TM has many causes because there are so many possible antigens. The inflammation that causes such extensive damage to nerve fibers of the spinal cord may result from viral infections, abnormal immune reactions, or insufficient blood flow through the blood vessels located in the spinal cord. Transverse myelitis also may occur as a complication of syphilis, measles, Lymes disease, and some vaccinations, including those for chickenpox and rabies. Cases in which a cause cannot be identified are called *idiopathic*.

Trigeminal Neuralgia (TN)

Inflammation of the 5th Cranial Nerve with pain in the cheek or head, called Trigeminal Neuralgia or *tic douloureux*. The pain causes sudden, twitching, burning or shock-like face pain that lasts a second or two followed by a pain free interval for a few minutes and can continue to reoccur in episodes. The intensity of pain can become incapacitating. TN pain is typically felt on one side of the jaw or cheek. Episodes last for days, or weeks at a time and then can reoccur later. In the days before an episode begins, some patients may experience a tingling or numbing sensation or a somewhat constant and aching pain. The attacks often worsen over time.

The pain can be triggered by vibration or contact with the cheek (such as when shaving, washing the face) brushing teeth, eating, drinking, talking, or being exposed to the wind. TN occurs in people over age 50, and is more common in women than in men.

A more complete list of Autoimmune Diseases:

- Achlorhydra Autoimmune Active Chronic Hepatitis
- Addison's Disease
- Alopecia Areata
- Amyotrophic Lateral Sclerosis (ALS, Lou Gehrig's Disease)
- Ankylosing Spondylitis
- Anti-GBM Nephritis or anti-TBM Nephritis
- Antiphospholipid Syndrome
- Aplastic Anemia
- Arthritis
- Asthma
- Atopic Allergy
- Atopic Dermatitis
- Autoimmune Inner Ear Disease (AIED)
- Autoimmune Lymphoproliferative Syndrome (ALPS)
- Balo Disease
- Behcet's Disease
- Berger's Disease (IgA Nephropathy)
- Bullous Pemphigoid
- Cardiomyopathy
- Celiac Disease
- Chronic Fatigue Immune Dysfunction Syndrome (CFIDS)
- Churg Strauss Syndrome
- Cicatricial Pemphigoid
- Cogan's Syndrome
- Cold Agglutunin Disease
- Colitis
- Cranial Arteritis
- CREST Syndrome
- Crohn's Disease
- Cushing's Syndrome
- Dego's Disease
- Dermatitis

- Dermatomyositis
- Devic Disease
- Diabetes, Type 1
- Diabetes, Type 2
- Dressler's Syndrome
- Discoid Lupus
- Eczema
- Essential Mixed Cryoglobulinemia
- Eosinophilic Fasciitis
- Epidermolysis Bullosa Acquisita
- Evan's Syndrome
- Fibromyalgia
- Fibromyositis
- Fibrosing Alveolitis
- Gastritis
- Giant Cell Artertis
- Glomerulonephritis
- Goodpasture's Disease
- Grave's Disease
- Guillian-Barre Syndrome
- Hashimoto's Thyroiditis
- Hemolytic Anemia
- Henoch-Schonlein Purpura
- Hepatitis
- Hughes Syndrome
- Idiopathic Adrenal Atrophy
- Idiopathic Pulmonary Fibrosis
- Idiopathic Thrombocytopenia Purpura
- Inflammatory Demylinating Polyneuropathy
- Irritable Bowel Syndrome
- Kawasaki's Disease
- Lichen Planus
- Lou Gehrig's Disease
- Lupoid Hepatitis
- Lupus
- Lymes Disease
- Meniere's Disease
- Mixed Connective Tissue Disease
- Multiple Myeloma

- Multiple Sclerosis
- Myasthenia Gravis
- Myositis
- Ocular Cicatricial Pemphigoid
- Osteoporosis
- Pars Planitis
- Pemphigus Vulgaris
- Polyglandular Autoimmune Syndromes
- Polymyalgia Rheumatica (PMR)
- Polymyositis
- Primary Biliary Cirrhois
- Primary Sclerosing Cholangitis
- Psoriasis
- Raynaud's Phenomenon
- Reiter's Syndrome
- Rheumatic Fever
- Rheumatoid Arthritis
- Sarcoidosis
- Scleritis
- Scleroderma
- Sjogren's Syndrome
- Sticky Blood Syndrome
- Still's Disease
- Stiff Man Syndrome
- Sydenham Chorea
- Systemic Lupus Erythmatosis (SLE)
- Takayasu's Arteritis
- Temporal Arteritis
- Ulcerative Colitis
- Vasculitis
- Vitiligo
- Wegener's Granulomatosis
- Wilson's Syndrome

Chapter Two

Diagnosing Autoimmune Disorders

"All political (may I add medical) thinking for years past has been vitiated in the same way. People can foresee the future only when it coincides with their own wishes, and the most grossly obvious facts can be ignored when they are unwelcome."

George Orwell

How do you know if a patient is autoimmune? Are there some clinical 'hints' that should tip the practitioner or signs that should make a person question? I've listed a few signals that, if you notice you fit into one or more of these, it may be a good idea to get some testing done:

1. You already suffer from a known autoimmune disorder (RA, psoriasis, ulcerative colitis, Type 1 diabetes, Sjorgen's syndrome, scleroderma, sarcoidosis, lupus, Hashimotos….you get the picture). If you already have another autoimmune disease, the chances are higher that current symptoms in a seemingly unrelated area may be from an attack to that tissue as well.
2. Your symptoms wax and wane. This is classic with autoimmune disease. Remember, it is when the immune attack occurs that you usually feel the worse so when your Th1 or Th2 system is

'ramped up', the inflammation is highest and your symptoms worsen. As time passes, your immune system may fatigue and ironically, when your immune system is completely 'pooped out' is when you feel better, you think that you may be on the road to recovery only to be knocked back down once your body has rested and gotten 'back to the fight'.

3. You take a boatload of supplements. I've had patients bring in bags of supplements that they've tried, are trying, or read about and plan to start. Usually autoimmune patients are desperate, they are searching, have not received much support or have run into a salesman who peddled them stuff they just don't need. There is a serious danger here as well. Remember that certain supplements stimulate a Th1 response and others stimulate a Th2 response. If you are Th1 dominant and you are taking Th1 stimulants, you are feeding the fire! You may as well drink poison!

4. Life fell apart for you after _____. This is a very common finding in the history of the case; events in life ramp the immune system and can cause it to recognize a latent antigen that has lain dormant for years. I liken it to your home in a quite neighborhood. You like your neighbors and never noticed anything wrong or unusual until the day that the city doubled the police force and added security for the upcoming political event next month. When you came home from work there were four police cars next door and they were hauling thugs out in handcuffs from the crack house no one knew was there. Events in life, whether emotional, physical or spiritual, can cause a rise in the immune response, an increase in security that may flush out things lodged in tissues for years. Well, if this added security recognizes an antigen that isn't alive and won't die, the immune response is 'turned on' and the autoimmune disease is set in motion.

5. Following pregnancy. A pregnant woman normally will be Th2 dominant in her third trimester and then Th1 dominant post partum. I often hear comments like, "I always felt best being pregnant, if I could only stay in a pregnant state, my life would be great;" or, "I love my kids but pregnancy just killed me, it was the worst I ever felt." The one who felt great during pregnancy was the autoimmune patient who was Th1

dominant. When in the third trimester their body swung to Th2 dominant, it was a temporary balancing that dramatically improved symptoms and they felt great. Usually this same patient suffered post partum depression due to the violent swing in the other direction after giving birth. The opposite was true for the mother who hated being pregnant. She was Th2 dominant already and the Th2 swing in the third trimester just made her worse; boy was she a happy momma once the baby came and she just couldn't figure out why those other moms struggled with depression and exhaustion.
6. Positive testing via immune panels. (see below) Ultimately you want to get tested.

I. Autoimmune testing. The typical testing for autoimmune diagnosis is antibody testing. If Hashimoto's is suspected, protocol dictates we run TPO antibodies and if positive, it would be a definite confirmation of our diagnosis. The only problem with antibody testing is that if a patient is Th1 dominant, they will be suppressing the Th2 system that makes the antibodies. Many patients that truly are autoimmune patients have negative antibody tests due to Th1 dominance and the diagnosis is missed! A more accurate testing is Cytokine tests. These will prove an autoimmune reaction AND show which side is dominant!

II. Antigen Testing. There are many sources for testing antigens. Blood tests will only reveal what is circulating in the blood at the time of the draw so it is unreliable. Hair analysis for heavy metals is reliable but samples must be done correctly without coloring, harsh shampoos and other hair products, etc. A technique called Applied Kinesiology is reliable and one we use for screening toxins but it must be done by a professional with a lot of experience in the art. Enterolab is a laboratory that created the most reliable testing for food based toxins and genetic testing for such. We run the Enterolab test for gluten, soy, casein, egg, and yeast on every patient with a suspected autoimmune disorder. We run a Stool Microbial Ecology Profile as well. This test, by Metametrix Labs, will reveal intestinal parasites.

III. Complete Blood Panels (LabCorp or your local lab)

We need a Complete Metabolic Panel, a Lipid panel, a Thyroid panel

(TSH, free T3, Free T4, and Total T3), a CBC with auto differential, C-reactive protein, homocysteine, TIBC, and 25-OH Vitamin D as well as 1, 25-OH Vitamin D levels. We recommend that you run the TPO and TGB antibodies or other antibodies specific to the area of attack even though they may not be positive if the patient is Th1 dominant.

The main priorities when looking at the blood work are:

- Autoimmune diagnosis, antigen detection and immune system dominance
- Anemias present: Iron, B12, Vitamin D, Pernicious, and Folic Acid
- Blood sugar/Insulin balance within functional ranges
- Adrenal function and hypothalamus-pituitary axis health
- Liver congestion, and health of detoxification pathways
- Gastrointestinal tract health, Leaky Gut, Metabolic Toxic Bowel, Probiotic health, Stomach health, Hypochlorhydria, H Pylori infections, ulcerations
- Cell membrane health, Bio-Impedance test, fatty acid metabolism
- Thyroid health – complete thyroid panels
- Inflammatory states, possible cancer markers, toxicities
- Other pathologies, genetic markers, genetic predominance

IV. Adrenal Stress Index (ASI) from www.diagnostechs.com:

We run this test on everyone simply due to the fact that stress is ubiquitous in this country. If there is any chronic fatigue, brain imbalances, hormone issues, blood sugar problems, etc., adrenal fluctuations may be evident. The ASI measures cortisol output throughout the day.

V. Immune Panels:

1. Immune Dysregulation: Th1/Th2 out of balance

Th1 and Th2 → which is dominant? If NO autoimmune disorder → neither is!

Th1 Dom = high IL-2, IL-12, NKC and TNF-alpha
Th1 is T-cells. T-cells are the police force that attacks and cleans up

afterward. (Helper T-cells, Suppressor T-cells, NKC, regulatory T-cells, and macrophages).

Th2 Dom = high IL-4, IL-13 and IL-10
Th2 is B-cells. B-cells make anti-bodies. They tell T-cells what to kill. If the testing comes back with a high B-cell count, the patient is Th2 dominant.

2. Active Antigen vs. Dysregulation.

Active antigens are BIOtoxins → parasites, bacteria, virus, mold, yeast, fungi, or protozoan → that your body is trying to KILL right NOW, NOT an autoimmune response to them; this is a BIG DIFFERENCE. If your immune system is simply killing an Antigen, then aid the high immune pattern (if high Th1, help increase it). BUT, if it is autoimmune toxicity, then treat as an autoimmune condition, NOT a normal physiologic response!!!!

The best indicator for an active antigen as the cause of the patient's abnormal dominance is the "Helper/Suppressor" ratio on the T & B cell panel. (Also called "CD4:CD8" ratio).

The closer to 2.5 the ratio is (or if above that), the more likely it is that you're dealing with an Active Antigen. If the ratio is below 1.2, then you are most likely dealing with a dys-regulation problem.

If ACTIVE ANTIGEN = treat accordingly!!

To test for active antigens use the following tests:

1. Metametrix.com = Stool Microbial Ecology Profile #2105
2. Enterolab.com for food antigens
3. Urea/H.Pylori breathe test from Metsol.com

VI. Intestinal Permeability from www.genovadiagnostics.com:

LGS or Leaky gut syndrome describes a condition of altered or damaged bowel lining, caused by antibiotics, toxins, poor diet, parasites or infection can lead to increased permeability of the gut wall to toxins, microbes, undigested food, waste or larger than normal macromolecules. It has been proposed that these substances affect the body directly, while others postulate an immune reaction to these substances.

VII. HORMONE PANELS from www.diagnostechs.com:

We can check hormone panels to determine if the patient suffers from low testosterone in males or low/hi estrogen/progesterone levels in females. Symptoms related to decreased hormone levels may include depression, fatigue, mental fogginess, mood swings, hot flashes, sweating attacks, weight gain, and decreased physical stamina. We ONLY run what are called Expanded Panels. These are panels that take a 'movie' over an entire cycle for the female. It does little good to see a snapshot of hormonal activity; we need the entire cycle to measure fluctuations.

VIII. Urea / H. Pylori from www.metsol.com:

We run the only reliable test for H. Pylori bacteria to determine any problems related to the gut function. This is a breathe test, not a blood test.

IX. Homocysteine and C-reactive protein:

Testing for inflammation. Tested through LabCorp or your local lab.

We cannot overemphasize the importance of homocysteine and C-reactive protein testing. Homocysteine levels are toxic in functionally high concentrations and responsible for the etching of the arteriole walls that lead to atherosclerosis. C-reactive protein is a measurement of inflammation in the body and may be the first indicator of an autoimmune response.

X. Additional Thyroid Testing:

Understanding Thyroid Markers and Panels

TSH: Thyroid Stimulating Hormone (TSH) is also called thyrotropin. The pituitary releases this hormone after the hypothalamus releases TRH (thyrotropin-releasing-hormone). This is the most common marker used to assess thyroid function and it is also the most sensitive. The TSH levels increase when the T4 levels drop, and the TSH falls when T4 levels increase. This is the only test performed in the traditional health care model as a means to screen the patient for thyroid disorders; this is because they are only concerned for screening the thyroid for hormone replacement and not optimal physiological function. A TSH test alone does not consider thyroid-pituitary feedback loops, peripheral thyroid metabolism, or potential or active risk factors as identified by antibody testing. A high TSH with or without changes in T4 or T3 is diagnostic to determine hypothyroidism. If the thyroid is not making enough T4 the pituitary will pump out TSH to stimulate its production. A low TSH is used to determine hyperthyroid activity. If the thyroid is overactive, such as in Grave's disease, the antibodies bind to active thyrotropin (TSH) receptors on the thyroid cells and stimulate T4 production without the influence of TSH. Please note that some antibodies may inhibit thyroid function by inactivating instead of stimulating thyrotropin receptors. This is called an autoimmune hypothyroid. These patterns will demonstrate a hypothyroid pattern (elevated TSH) with elevated thyroid antibodies.

Laboratory Reference Range: 0.5 – 5.5 (varies from one lab to another)

Functional or Optimal Reference Range: 1.5 – 3.5

Total Thyroxine (TT4): The TT4 test measures both bound and unbound Thyroxine levels. Therefore, it does not give the activity of T4 when measured alone. This test is best completed with a T3 uptake. The free Thyroxine index (FT4) can be calculated by using the T3 uptake and demonstrate a level of T4 activity. Total T4 levels can be altered by many drugs (see Category of drugs that interfere with thyroid activity).

Functional Reference Range: 6-12 ug/d

Free Thyroxine Index: As stated earlier, the total Thyroxine and the T3 uptake must be used together to calculate the FT4. The index is measured by multiplying the TT4 levels by the T3 uptake levels. The result is the FT4 and it determines the amount of active T4 available. The impact of drugs, as will be discussed, will always impact T4 and resin T3 uptake levels in opposite directions due to their impact on binding sites. If the TT4 level is depressed, then the T3 uptake is high; if the TT4 is elevated, the resin uptake is low. Please note that even if you are taking drugs that may impact thyroid binding, the free Thyroxine index should be within the normal range if your thyroid is functioning normally.

Functional Reference Range: 1.2 -4.9 ml/dl

Free Thyroxine (FT4): The free Thyroxine test is used to measure the amount of free or active T4 in the blood. All the factors such as drugs and physical conditions that may impact the TT4 do not impact the FT4. The level of T4 in the blood is high with hyperthyroidism or low with hypothyroidism. Please note that even a TSH with normal T4 is enough to diagnose hypothyroidism. A rare pattern is an elevated T4 without hyperthyroidism which may be related to a hereditary condition of thyroid resistance. Elevated free T4 may also be caused by patients taking heparin or by an acute illness that may briefly cause the binding protein levels to suddenly fall. If an illness becomes severe and chronic it may decrease the FT4 levels but it is not a thyroid disease.

Functional Reference Range: 1.0 -1.5 ng/dL

Resin T3 Uptake: The resin T3 uptake measures the amount of sites for active (unbound) T3 to bind with Thyroxine binding proteins. This test is performed by mixing the blood with radioactive thyroid hormones. These radioactive hormones then combine with binding sites on Thyroxine-binding proteins. The blood is then exposed to a substance called a resin which will bind the unbound thyroid hormones and measure for radioactivity. The result can be expressed as the percent of radioactivity found on the resin, compared to the original radioactivity that was added. The more binding sites that are open on the proteins, the lower the resin uptake result will be, and vice versa. For example, anything that reduces the binding sites, such as elevated testosterone or testosterone replacement therapy, can cause a low T4 measurement because it leaves very few binding sites for any thyroid hormone to bind to. If T3 is added to the sample of the blood, little T3 will be bound. This pattern would have low TT4 levels and high resin T3 uptake levels. On the other hand, anything that raises the binding sites such as estrogen or birth control pills would cause a pattern of high TT4 and low T3 uptake.

Functional Reference Range: 28-38 mg/dl

Free Triiodothyronine (FT3): This test measures the free T3 hormone levels. This test is rarely completed in traditional endocrinology. It is typically only used in a situation when a patient has hyperthyroid, yet the FT4 levels are normal. However, the FT3 test is the best marker for measuring the amount of active thyroid hormones available for the thyroid receptor sites.

Functional Reference Range: 300-400 pg/ml

Reverse T3 (rT3): This test measures the amount of reverse T3 that is produced. The production of rT3 typically takes place in cases of extreme stress, such as major trauma, surgery or severe chronic stress. It appears that the increased production of reverse T3 is due to an inability to clear rT3m as well as from elevated cortisol.

Functional Reference Range: 90-350 pg/ml

Thyroid Antibodies: Thyroid auto-antibodies indicate that the body's immune system is attacking itself. Production of thyroid auto-antibodies may create a hypothyroid or a hyperthyroid state. Some antibodies attach to the TSH receptors but do not cause a response; therefore, the patient will complain of low thyroid symptoms. However, the serum TSH may not be altered. It is just not able to cause a cellular change. On the other hand, some antibodies will bind to the receptor sites and cause over activation of the thyroid. This will present as elevated T4 levels, a low TSH, and elevated thyroid antibodies.

Dr. Kevin Conners

THE AUTOIMMUNE PAIN QUESTIONNAIRE

Please Read: This questionnaire is designed to enable us to understand how much your pain and/or symptoms have affected your ability to manage your everyday activities. Please answer each Section by Checking the **ONE CHOICE** that most applies to you. We realize that you may feel that more than one statement may relate to you, but **PLEASE JUST CHECK THE ONE CHOICE WHICH MOST CLOSELY DESCRIBES YOUR PROBLEM RIGHT NOW.**

NAME:_____DATE: _____

SECTION 1—Pain Intensity
❑ 0 My pain comes and goes and is very mild.
❑ 1 My pain is mild and does not vary much.
❑ 2 My pain comes and goes and it is moderate.
❑ 3 My pain is moderate and does not vary much.
❑ 4 My pain comes and goes and is severe.
❑ 5 My pain is severe and does not vary much.

SECTION 2—Fatigue
❑ 0 My fatigue comes and goes and is very mild.
❑ 1 My fatigue is mild and does not vary much.
❑ 2 My fatigue comes and goes and it is moderate.
❑ 3 My fatigue is moderate and does not vary much.
❑ 4 My fatigue comes and goes and it is severe.
❑ 5 My fatigue is severe and does not vary much.

SECTION 3----Personal Care
❑ 0 I would not have to change my way of washing or dressing in order to avoid symptoms.
❑ 1 I do not normally change my way of washing or dressing even though it causes some symptoms.
❑ 2 Washing and dressing increases symptoms, but I manage not to change my way of doing it.
❑ 3 Washing and dressing increase symptoms and I find it necessary to change my way of doing it.

❏ 4   Because of symptoms, I am unable to do some washing and dressing without help.
❏ 5   Because of symptoms, I am unable to do any washing or dressing without help.

SECTION 4—Lifting
❏ 0   I can lift heavy weights without extra symptoms.
❏ 1   I can lift heavy weights, but it causes extra symptoms.
❏ 2   Symptoms prevent me from lifting heavy weights off the floor.
❏ 3   Symptoms prevent me from lifting heavy weights off the floor but I can manage if they are conveniently positioned, e.g. on a table.
❏ 4   Symptoms prevent me from lifting heavy weights, but I manage light to medium
         weights if they are conveniently positioned.
❏ 5   I can only lift very light weights, at the most.

SECTION 5—Walking
❏ 0 Pain does not prevent me from walking any distance
❏ 1 Pain prevents me from walking more than one mile.
❏ 2 Pain prevents me from walking more than ½ mile.
❏ 3 Pain prevents me from walking ¼ mile.
❏ 4 I can only walk while using a cane or on crutches.
❏ 5 I am in bed most of the time and have to crawl to the toilet.

SECTION 6—Sitting
❏ 0 I can sit in any chair as long as I like without pain.
❏ 1 I can only sit in my favorite chair as long as I like.
❏ 2 Pain prevents me from sitting more than one hour.
❏ 3 Pain prevents me from sitting more than ½ hour.
❏ 4 Pain prevents me from sitting more than ten minutes.
❏ 5 Pain prevents me from sitting at all.

SECTION 7—Standing
❏ 0 I can stand as long as I want without pain.
❏ 1 I have some pain while standing, but it does not increase with time.

Dr. Kevin Conners

❏ 2 I cannot stand for longer than 1 hour without increasing pain.
❏ 3 I cannot stand for longer than 1/2 hour without increasing pain.
❏ 4 I cannot stand for longer then 10 minutes without increasing pain.
❏ 5 I avoid standing, because it increases the pain right away.

SECTION 8--Sleeping
❏ 0 I have no pain in bed.
❏ 1 I have pain in bed, but it does not prevent me from sleeping well.
❏ 2 Because of symptoms, my normal night's sleep is reduced by less than one-quarter.
❏ 3 Because of symptoms, my normal night's sleep is reduced by less than one-half.
❏ 4 Because of symptoms, my normal night's sleep is reduced by less than three-quarters.
❏ 5 My symptoms prevent me form sleeping at all.

SECTION 9—Gastro-Intestinal
❏ 0 I have no problems with my GI tract.
❏ 1 I have mild problems with gas, bloating, constipation and/or diarrhea.
❏ 2 I have mild/moderate problems with gas, bloating, constipation and/or diarrhea.
❏ 3 I have moderate problems with gas, bloating, constipation, and/or diarrhea.
❏ 4 I have moderate to severe problems with gas, bloating, constipation, and/or diarrhea.
❏ 5 I have severe problems with gas, bloating, constipation, and/or diarrhea.

SECTION 9—Social Life
❏ 0 My social life is normal and gives me no pain.
❏ 1 My social life is normal, but increases the degree of pain.
❏ 2 Pain has no significant effect on my social life apart from limiting my more
energetic interests, e.g. dancing, etc.

❏ 3 Pain has restricted my social life and I do not go out very often.
❏ 4 Pain has restricted my social life to my home.
❏ 5 I have hardly any social life because of the pain.

SECTION 10--Traveling
❏ 0   I get no pain while traveling.
❏ 1   I get some pain while traveling, but none of my usual forms of travel make it any worse.
❏ 2   I get extra pain while traveling but it does not compel me to seek alternate forms of travel.
❏ 3   I get extra pain while traveling which compels me to seek alternative forms of travel.
❏ 4   Pain restricts all forms of travel except that done lying down.
❏ 5   Pain restricts all forms of travel.

SECTION 11—Changing Degree of Pain
❏ 0 My pain is rapidly getting better
❏ 1 My pain fluctuates, but overall is definitely getting better.
❏ 2 My pain seems to be getting better, but improvement is slow at present.
❏ 3 My pain is neither getting better or worse.
❏ 4 My pain is gradually worsening.
❏ 5 My pain is rapidly worsening.

SECTION 12—Changing Degree of Fatigue
❏ 0 My fatigue is rapidly getting better
❏ 1 My fatigue fluctuates, but overall is definitely getting better.
❏ 2 My fatigue seems to be getting better, but improvement is slow at present.
❏ 3 My fatigue is neither getting better or worse.
❏ 4 My fatigue is gradually worsening.
❏ 5 My fatigue is rapidly worsening.

Chapter Three

Treating Autoimmune Disorders

"Anyone who proposes to do good must not expect people to roll stones out of his way, but must accept his lot calmly, even if they roll a few stones upon it."

Dr. Albert Schweitzer

Treatment

How do you treat autoimmune conditions? That is the question of the day! We will assume that we have identified the antigen, identified the Th1 / Th2 dominance, understood all of the body's adaptive processes taking place in the cardiovascular, gastrointestinal, eliminatory, hormonal, and neurological systems. We've also identified problems in fuel delivery systems to the cells, cell membrane and receptor site health, nutrient deficiencies, absorption and utilization problems, developmental disturbances and the like. Are there brain-based imbalances, cerebellar deficiencies, neurotransmitter imbalances? These need to be addressed. The autoimmune patient MUST be treated in a very holistic manner because of the intimate interconnections of all the systems. There is a delicate interpersonal relationship between everything that goes on in the body – you cannot separate the systems.

Where we have failed in treatment of patients and not achieved the level of success desired has ALWAYS been in this – we didn't look at everything at the same time. You have to get all the tests done! Look at everything; leave no stone unturned, don't assume anything!

Obviously, the first and arguably the most important piece of the treatment program involves getting rid of the antigen. If it's a food, stop eating it; if a chemical seek out possible exposures and limit that, if a biotoxin, look at exposures. Once present exposures are eliminated we need to detoxify the antigens that you have currently lodged in your tissues. This is a process that takes time and is specific to the antigen in question.

Detoxification

Everyone wants to know if they are toxic; it's a question that is answered with proper testing. Heavy metals and chemicals collectively are often referred to as xenobiotics (Gk. Xeno = foreign; biotics = bodies). This is an even more important question to answer as far as autoimmune disorders are concerned. We will examine a number of ways that we may test for different toxicities; some we have already covered, but first let's get a basic understanding of how it is possible to measure these xenobiotics in the body.

There are a variety of complex and sophisticated measuring instruments called spectrometers such as ICP-MS, ICP-OES, AF and GC-MS that can be used to measure the levels of xenobiotics in blood, urine, feces, hair, sweat and other body tissues. First, let's begin with a blanket statement that is important to understand:

**THERE IS NO WAY OF DETERMINING
THE TOTAL TOXIC LOAD IN A LIVING HUMAN!**

We mentioned LIVING HUMAN here, as it is possible to determine the total load of xenobiotics in a dead human – you would simply incinerate the person and measure the total load of xenobiotics in the ashes! We have yet to have a patient volunteer for this study.

Some in the medical field believe that serum testing revealing toxicity is a measurement of toxic load. Serum testing only reveals what is circulating in the blood at the time of the draw; it does not measure what is lodged in the tissue and the volume lodged in the tissue is the problem in autoimmune conditions. Serum and/or urine testing simply measures acute exposure! They also believe that they can measure the effectiveness of a chelating agent – for example, they take a chelating agent for x months and re-measure the amount of toxin in the blood or urine. If it decreases, they believe the treatment is working – hogwash! Time passed and the level of toxicity in the measured specimen has changed but we have no way of knowing if it exited the body or was deposited in the patient's frontal lobe.

When measuring toxins in the blood or urine, the first pre-sample is taken; this will tell us whether there are metals that are CIRCULATING in the blood and/or being filtered through the kidneys into the urine. If a reading of zero comes back from the lab, this does not mean that the person does not have metals STORED in their body tissues and organs – it simply means that there are no active metals running around the blood. Generally the body does not like these lethal toxins in the blood, so stores them in body tissues at the earliest opportunity. In order to determine whether there are metals STORED in the tissues and organs, another type of test has to be conducted using hair, feces, or Kinesiological means.

To determine what is being eliminated from the body's organs and tissues we can do a challenge test where we use a chelating agent that has the ability to "push-out" the metals into the blood where they can be collected in the urine – the post-sample. If indeed our chelating agent is doing this, then we would get a percentage increase of metals in this post-sample, compared to the pre-sample, taken before using the chelating agent. This is simply a brief of the complexities of biochemical testing and can help to determine whether a chelating agent is working or not.

Dr Georgio's research has shown conclusively that HMD™ (Heavy Metal Detox product that he sells) is an effective chelating agent for eliminating many different metals, and possibly other xenobiotics. There are other well-known chelators (EDTA and DMSA) for detoxing chemicals that need to be used with caution. This is why I am strongly against nutritionists peddling detoxification kits to people – if not monitored properly, herbal detoxification agents and chelators can simply circulate toxins out of tissues into the blood to be deposited at another site. This makes the patient sicker than before they started! Proper testing and case management must be done. These tests are expensive for the patients and their interpretation requires the wisdom of an experienced practitioner. Should everyone get tested and go through the expense or is it better to just assume you have xenotoxins? Rule number one – NEVER guess! One can use the pre-post provocation testing described above, hair analysis and blood work described in chapter 2, or the help of a skilled

Kinesiologist. Regardless, there are issues of sensitivity and downfalls of each testing procedure.

Personally, as a clinician we use both kinesiology and laboratory testing; I prefer to be doubly certain when ever possible. One could argue that EVERYONE is toxic, so it really is a decision between getting the patient to run expensive tests only to conclude that they are toxic and require chelation anyway, but I think it is CRUCIAL to know EXACTLY what toxin you are dealing with. This is NOT something to play around with and honestly, I had reservations in writing this book because of this fact alone – there are those who will experiment themselves in treating their own autoimmune case just to save a few bucks! Well hear me – I do NOT advocate this practice and this book, as well as my seminars, are NOT to educate the patient so they can treat themselves. I desire to bring knowledge into a field darkened by ignorance so people are empowered to seek help in the right direction. If you try to treat your own autoimmune disorder without the skilled guidance of a trusted practitioner, then I wash my hands of you case. I know this sounds mean but I have just seen too many horror stories in 25 years of practice.

Is Everyone Toxic?

In September 2005, Greenpeace International with the World Wildlife Fund published a document entitled, "Present for Life: Hazardous Chemicals in Umbilical Cord Blood." The research was a real eye-opener as it showed convincingly that newborns tested for hundreds of different toxins showed high levels of numerous toxins. Specifically, the blood tests showed that these newborns had an average of 287 toxins in their bodies, 180 of these are known carcinogens.

This study was conducted in America where the level of toxicity is arguably getting higher every year. A similar study conducted on pregnant women living in the North Pole which most people feel is a clean part of the earth. The research was published in The Science of the Total Environment that showed high concentrations of heavy metals, such as mercury, and organochlorines in the blood and fatty tissue of the Inuit Indians. This is attributed in part to their high consumption of the meat and blubber of marine mammals. In this study, 180 pregnant women and 178 newborn babies were studied, amounting to 36% of the total number of births in the Disko Bay area during 1994-1996.

Pesticides were found in the high concentrations in maternal blood, as were concentrations of organochlorines, mercury and selenium. Concentrations of mercury and cadmium increased with the consumption of marine mammals, and cadmium was associated with smoking. The contaminants are potentially toxic for several organ systems but the high concentrations of pollutants have so far not been shown to influence health as far as pathology is concerned. This means that no one's death has yet been attributed to the higher level of toxicity in our overall environment. The problem is in WHAT the toxicity does to us; it becomes an antigen that kills us slowly by diseases we call Diabetes, Heart Disease and Cancer. Similar studies have also shown that wildlife is also being killed due to high levels of toxic chemicals in their environment. One study showed that several arctic mammal and bird species that indicate chemical exposures are likely adversely affecting the health of these species. Some of the effects seen are potentially quite serious (e.g. immune suppression, hormone disturbances, altered behavior).

A further study published in the journal Environmental Research has shown that there is a correlation between the levels of methylmercury in the pregnant and lactating mother's blood and urine and that of her newborn child. It is clear that toxins from the mother can pass through the placenta and the baby. Another study published in 2001 in Neuro Toxicology showed that the level of mercury in baby's hair was quite high and argues that this is probably a consequence of vaccinations that contain mercury.

There is a lot of research indicating the health effects of high mercury levels on children, including the relationship of these chemical toxins to the levels of mercury found in adults due to amalgam fillings and there is further conclusive evidence that "we are all toxic."

We can all search the internet for ample proof of environmental toxicities that have invaded our food supplies and our bodies, but just because a person may have a toxic substance in their body does not necessarily mean they should attempt to detoxify it. Sometimes it may be best to 'let a sleeping dog lie.' It is when the toxin is recognized by the body that issues arise. This is how a heavy metal, that was present in a person's brain since 2 years of age, suddenly causes depression and panic attacks at 40 years old. The metal may not have been recognized by the body and never elicited an immune response until something seemingly unrelated caused the body to fire an immune response against the metal that has now become an antigen. This inflammatory, autoimmune attack must now be addressed!

Toxicologists studying chemical toxicity usually have a reference range of values which indicate the "safe levels" of these chemicals. New research is showing, however, that even low-dose exposure is accumulative over time and can lead to children having decreased performance in areas of motor function and memory. Similarly, disruption of attention, fine motor function and verbal memory was also found in adults on exposure to low mercury levels.

Mercury has been found to be a causative agent of various sorts of disorders, including neurological, nephrological (kidneys), immunological, cardiac, motor, reproductive and even genetic. Recently heavy metal mediated toxicity has been linked to diseases like Alzheimer's, Parkinson's, Autism, Lupus, ALS, etc.

Mercury Fillings

Mercury used in amalgam tooth fillings is a big issue of contention. Amalgam was found to be a cheap and long lasting substance to fill teeth with, but the danger of mercury poison was overlooked or ignored. The use of amalgams is now prohibited in many – though not all – countries. Dr. Engel, a holistic dentist, has written an interesting paper on the "Health Observations Before and After Amalgam Removal" The International Academy of Oral Medicine and Toxicology has produced a very interesting video describing the amount of mercury that is released from amalgam fillings, even though they may be over 30 years old. Chewing gum, drinking hot drinks and brushing teeth can increase the amount of methyl mercury released from amalgam fillings. If you ever have doubt about how lethal mercury is for the nervous system, and particularly the brain, you have to see the video produced by the University of Calgary, Faculty of Medicine, Department of Physiology and Biophysics – it clearly shows how mercury completely degenerates neural fibers in a Petri dish in zero time – it's a fascinating video to watch!

Vaccinations

The drugs used in vaccines and inoculations have for many years used mercury and aluminum as preservatives. There is an interesting article published in Medical hypotheses entitled, "Autism: A Novel Form of Mercury Poisoning'"" showing how exposure to mercury can cause immune, sensory, neurological, motor, and behavioral dysfunctions similar to traits defining or associated with autism. Although Thimerosal (the mercury preservative) has been phased out of many vaccinations, the effect – because it is cumulative and stays in the body – is with almost all adults today. The problem is that the heavy metals are not the only toxin in the vaccination. Service personnel who are subjected to many different injections for their tours of duty are particularly at risk from toxic poisoning.

The point is that toxicity is ubiquitous; we can run, but we cannot hide. Treatment MUST be based on identifying the specific antigen, getting it out of the body, calming the immune dysregulation, and balancing the other dysfunctional systems. There is no easy way around it and it should NOT be attempted without a skilled practitioner to help guide the way.

Dr. Kevin Conners

Diets we use as handouts

Eating God's Way

This is a general diet I use in our office. It is a good Diet for everyone!

Meat (grass-fed organic)
- meat bone soup or stock
- liver and heart (must be organic)
- lamb, buffalo, elk, venison, beef, goat, veal
- jerky (with no chemicals, nitrates, or nitrites)
- beef or buffalo sausage (with no pork casing)
- beef or buffalo hot dogs (with no pork casing)

> **NO Pork, scale-less fish, shellfish, shrimp, lobster or 'bottom-feeders'. Read Lev. 11**

Fish (wild- caught ONLY, and the <u>fish must be fish with fins and scales</u>. Eg: No catfish)
- fish soup or stock, salmon, halibut, tuna, cod, scrod, grouper, haddock, mahi-mahi, pompano, Wahoo
- trout, orange roughy, sea bass, snapper, sardines (canned in water or olive oil only), herring, sole, whitefish

Poultry (pastured, free-range and organic)
- poultry bone soup or stock, chicken, Cornish game hen, guinea fowl, turkey, duck
- chicken or turkey bacon or sausage (with no pork casing)

Lunch Meat (organic, free range, and hormone free ONLY)
- turkey, chicken, roast beef

Eggs (high omega-3/DHA or organic is best)
- chicken eggs (whole with yolk) <u>UNLESS</u> Egg intolerant

Dairy (organic and UN-Pasteurized (RAW) ONLY – NON if Dairy Intolerant!!!!)
- Really NO Dairy for everyone is BEST!!!!!!!!!!!!!
- homemade kefir made from raw goat's milk or raw cow's milk
- raw goat's milk hard cheeses, raw cow's milk hard cheeses
- goat's milk plain whole yogurt, organic cow's milk yogurt or kefir

- raw cream, raw butter

Fats and Oils (organic is best)
- Oil: coconut oil, extra virgin (best for cooking) olive oil,
- Spread: Ghee butter; RAW butter
- avocado, coconut milk/cream (canned), oil,

Vegetables (organic fresh or frozen is best)
- ALL veggies – especially lower carb, organic (broccoli, artichokes, asparagus, beets, cauliflower)
- Brussels sprouts, cThlge, squash (winter or summer), carrots, celery, cucumbers, eggplant, pumpkins
- Garlic, onions, leafy greens (kale, collard, broccoli, mustard greens)
- salad greens (radicchio, escarole, endive), okra, lettuce (leafs of all kinds), spinach, mushrooms, peas
- peppers, string beans, tomatoes, sprouts (broccoli, sunflower, pea shoots, radish, etc.)
- sweet potatoes, sea vegetables (kelp, dulse, nori, kombu, and hijiki),
- STRICTLY LIMIT white potatoes and corn

> *"You shall walk after the Lord your God and [reverently] fear Him, and keep His commandments and obey His voice, and you shall serve Him and cling to Him."* Dt 13:4

Fruits (organic fresh or frozen is best)
- Stone fruits are BEST – fruits with a pit
- Blueberries, strawberries, blackberries, raspberries, lemons, limes, apples, apricots, grapes, melons
- Peaches, oranges, grapefruit, pears, plums, kiwis, pineapples, bananas, mangos, papayas
- dried fruits (no sugar or sulfites), raisins, figs, dates, prunes

Grains and Starchy Carbohydrates (organic is best, and whole grains and flours are best if soaked for six to twelve hours before cooking)
<u>Brain-Based Therapy patients MUST stay off Gluten!!!</u>
- <u>Gluten-FREE</u> oats, rice, millet
- Pamela's Mix brand flour for baking, waffles, pancakes
- UDI bread is a good gluten free brand that makes bread and muffins

Sweeteners

- Unheated raw honey; honey; date sugar; stevia; pure maple syrup; NO ARTIFICIAL SWEETNERS!!!!!!

Beans and Legumes (best if soaked for twelve hours)
- miso, lentils, tempeh, natto, black beans, kidney beans, navy beans, white beans, pinto beans, red beans
- split peas, garbanzo beans, lima beans, broad beans, black-eyed peas

Nuts and Seeds (organic, raw, and/or soaked is best)
- RAW almonds, pumpkin seeds, hemp seeds, flaxseeds, sunflower seeds, almond butter, tahini,
- hemp or pumpkin seed butter, sunflower butter, walnuts, macadamia nuts, pecans, hazelnuts, Brazil nuts

Condiments, Spices, and Seasonings (organic is best – MUST BE GLUTEN FREE)
- salsa (fresh or canned), tomato sauce (no added sugar), guacamole (fresh), soy sauce (wheat free, tamari)
- apple cider vinegar, raw salad dressings and marinades, herbs and spices (no added stabilizers)
- Herbamare seasoning, Celtic Sea Salt, sea salt, mustard, ketchup (no sugar), salad dressings (no canola oil)
- marinades (no canola oil), omega-3 mayonnaise, natural extracts such as vanilla or almond

Snacks (organic is best – MUST BE GLUTEN FREE)
- healthy food bars (Designs for Health), Organic milk protein powder, Gluten-free crackers, raw food snacks
- healthy macaroons, healthy trail mix, organic cocoa powder, organic chocolate spreads, carob powder

Beverages
- Reverse osmosis purified water; unsweetened or honey-sweetened herbal teas
- raw vegetable or fruit juices, lacto-fermented beverages, coconut water

*Limit Carbohydrates to less than 75 grams/day or less than 50 grams per day if Glucose over 100
*Detox Diets I recommend may severely limit some of the above for a period of time
*Consider Coffee Enemas to flush out the intestinal tract and cleanse the body (NO if you are TH2 Dom)

Add ONLY supplements that Dr. Conners has instructed – never buy things from store!
Study and meditate on Scripture daily, focus on what is good, holy and righteous; keep away from the negative, bad thoughts and disease-oriented thinking. Focus on the PROCESS not the outcome.

1. You HAVE to eat breakfast and it MUST be a protein!
2. Become a grazer – eat multiple small meals throughout the day
3. Keep Carbohydrates to a minimum

Dr Conners' Metabolic Syndrome Diet -this is really a good diet for everyone!

Def: Metabolic Syndrome or Syndrome X is a condition where a patient has fasting glucose levels between 100 or above. I like to see fasting blood glucose levels between 85-90, anything creeping up past 90 prompts a person to follow this diet:

**Note – if this is a chronic condition, you MUST be checked for Autoimmune, pre-diabetes which changes this diet significantly!

Morning: With Metabolic Syndrome you MUST eat breakfast!!! It needs to be a high protein, low carbohydrate breakfast. You've just gone a long time since you ate last and your adrenal gland is going to 'kick-in' to get you going. It is very common for Metabolic Syndrome patients to get poor sleep or wake up at 3am and not be able to get back to sleep. This is due to an over-firing midbrain and adrenal gland. You need to calm down your system by eating a low carbohydrate, high protein and fat breakfast. Usually these patients have little or no appetite in the morning (they are flying off of adrenal hormones). No appetite and even nausea are symptoms of adrenal fatigue, the worst thing you can do is eat sugar and drink coffee! Force yourself to eat protein and fat.

Snacks: Eat small amounts of proteins frequently. It is best if you have some protein at each meal. It need not be a large amount at any one time. In fact, it is best if you stick to smaller amounts (< 2–4 ounces of meat, fish, foul, or eggs at a time). Both animal and vegetarian sources of protein are beneficial. Choose a variety of meat products and try to find the healthiest options available; i.e., free range, antibiotic free, and/or organic, whenever possible. Eggs for most people are an excellent source of protein. Eat the whole egg, the lecithin in the yolk is essential to lower blood fat and improve liver and brain function. With any protein, the way in which you prepare it is critical. (The closer to raw or rare the better as long as you have proper HCl production in your stomach – get it evaluated!). Remember, any time meats and vegetables are heated over 110° Fahrenheit; crucial enzymes are damaged and lost. Avoid frying. Grilled, boiled, steamed, soft boiled, or poached are best methods for preparing foods.

Vegetables: Eat more, more, more. This is the one area where most everyone can improve his/her diet, and it is an especially important area for you. Always look for a variety, although make the green leafy types your preference. This includes spinach, chard, beet greens, kale, broccoli, mustard greens, etc.

As stated above for proteins, the quality of your produce (fresh and organic preferred) and the method of preparation is critical. Raw is preferred with lightly steamed or sautéed as your second choice for all vegetables. Use only butter or olive oil to sauté. When eating salads try not to eat iceberg lettuce. Rather, use lettuces with a rich green color, sprouts and raw nuts. Don't make salads your only choice for vegetables.

Fruits: Most people wrongly try to drink their fruits. Fruit juice is loaded with the simple sugar fructose, which is shunted into forming triglycerides and ultimately stored as fat. Without the fiber in the fruit, juice sends a rapid burst of fructose into the blood stream. When you do eat fruit, only eat one type of fruit at a time on an empty stomach; second, avoid the sweetest fruits/tropical fruits, except papaya which is very rich in digestive enzymes (fruits from colder climates are preferred); and third, eat only the highest quality, fresh and organic when possible. With Metabolic Syndrome, stone fruits are best!

Carbohydrates: This is a very tricky area. Most people have one classification for carbohydrates when in reality there are really three different types — complex, simple, and processed. Unfortunately, for most patients suffering with **Metabolic Syndrome**, almost any carbohydrate is a no-no. It is a physiological fact that the more carbohydrates you eat the more you will want. Craving carbohydrates is a symptom of an imbalance, so you can use this craving to monitor your progress. Overall, <u>eat vegetables as your carbohydrate</u> choice and limit grains (even the whole grains can be trouble). When you do eat whole grains, take them in moderation (rice is best). If you start the day with carbohydrates, you are more likely to crave them throughout the day, and then you'll eat more and it's downhill from there. Absolutely stay away from gluten breads, muffins, cookies, candies, crackers, pastas, white rice and most baked goods.

If your 12 hour fasting glucose levels are above 110, I recommend that

you start COUNTING your CARBS! You should not go over 50 grams of carbs per day; that's pretty stiff so you better think of it like a bank account that you cannot go over! If you simply refuse to watch this little detail, you have Diabetes to look forward to, along with heart disease and kidney failure – good luck with that! Sorry to sound so nasty, but only YOU can make this decision.

There's another dark side to processed carbohydrates that isn't talked about much — the connection to weight gain, elevated cholesterol and triglycerides, heart disease, and cancer. You don't even need to know the details to get the idea how much trouble carbohydrates can be.

Grains: There has been a tremendous amount of debate regarding grains. Whole unprocessed grains can be rich sources of vitamins and minerals, but with soil depletion and the special strains of grain that modern agriculture has developed, it isn't clear what nutrients remain. The two predominantly used grains in this country are genetically engineered and have five times the gluten content and only 1/3 of the protein content of the original wheat from which they were derived. This high gluten content is to blame for many patients' allergic reactions. When scholars have studied disease patterns and the decline of various civilizations, many of the degenerative diseases developed when cultivation of grains became a major part of their diet. Chemicals naturally found in certain grains, lack of the appropriate enzymes, and the carbohydrate content of grains make them a source of trouble for many individuals. My opinion at this time is to **ELIMINATE ALL grains such as wheat, rye and barley** even if you are not gluten sensitive. Unprocessed, **gluten-free** oats and brown rice can be considered on occasion to give you more variety.

Sweeteners: Use only a *small* amount of pure maple syrup, raw Tupelo honey or Stevia as sweeteners. Absolutely NO Nutri-Sweet, other brand names of artificial sweeteners and high fructose corn syrup; limit corn syrup and table sugar. If you cheat, be smart and use only small amounts with a meal with added fiber but NEVER cheat with sugar substitutes!

Fats: Fats don't make you fat → they save your life! The bad news is you probably do not get enough of the right fats in your diet. So, please use olive oil (cold pressed, extra virgin), walnut oil, coconut oil and grape seed oils. These are all actually beneficial, as long as they are cold-pressed. When cooking, use only raw butter, coconut oil, and olive oil — they are the only three oils safe to cook with. Avoid all hydrogenated and partially hydrogenated fats. *They are poisons to your system.* Never eat margarine again. Also, avoid peanut butter (use different nut butters). Eat all the avocados and raw nuts you desire.

If you think eating fat will make you fat, think again. When you eat fat, a chemical signal is sent to your brain to slow down the movement of food out of your stomach. As a result, you feel full. It is not surprising that recent research is showing that those who eat "fat-free" products tend to actually consume more calories than those who eat foods that have not had their fat content reduced (low fat usually means high sugar/high calories). In addition, fats are used not only for energy, but also for building the membrane around every single cell in your body. Fats also play a role in the formation of hormones, which of course make you feel and function well. It is far worse to be hormone-depleted from a low fat diet than it is to overeat fat. The sickest patients we see are the ones who have been on a fat-free diet for a long period of time. Like carbohydrates, choose your fats wisely — this program is not suggesting fried or processed foods.

Milk Products

Milk Products: Forget *pasteurized* cow milk products (milk, certain cheeses, sour cream, half & half, ice cream, cottage cheese and yogurt). If you only knew all the potential problems from pasteurized milk, you'd swear it off forever. Milk is actually more detrimental than sugar for many people (man is the only mammal that continues to drink milk after weaning). Avoiding dairy products will make it much easier for you to attain your optimal level of health and hormonal balance. Raw butter and Kefir (liquid yogurt), however, are excellent sources of essential nutrients and vitamins. Raw milk cheese, goat and sheep cheeses and milk products are great alternatives because their genetic code and fat content appear to be more like those of humans.

There has been a lot of hype about using soy milk and rice milk to replace dairy products. They sound like healthy alternatives, but in reality, they are highly processed foods that are primarily simple carbohydrates. You're better off doing without these as well, especially the soy – it is horrible for women especially. Use hemp milk or almond milk, they are more complete proteins.

Liquids: Water is best, about a half to one gallon a day, and herbal tea. Avoid all soda. No coffees until you are fully recovered. Fruit juices are forbidden because of their high fructose content and dumping of sugar into the blood stream. An occasional small glass of vegetable juice with a meal is probably okay, but water really is best.

If you enjoy wine or beer and still insist, there are some guidelines. First, drink only with meals. Red wine has less sugar and more of the beneficial polyphenols than white wines. Most of the good foreign beer is actually brewed and contains far more nutrients than the pasteurized chemicals called beer made by the large commercial breweries in the United States. Trader Joe's usually has a good selection. Less is better. Because coffee and alcohol force you to lose water, you'll have to drink more water to compensate.

The most important life-giving substance in the body is water. The daily routine of the body depends on a turnover of about 40,000 glasses of water per day. In the process, your body loses a minimum of six glasses per day, even if you don't do anything. With movement, exercise, and sugar intake, etc., you can require up to over 15 glasses of water per day. Consider this: the concentration of water in your brain has been estimated to be 85% and the water content of your tissues like your liver, kidney, muscle, heart, intestines, etc. is 75%. The concentration of water outside of the cells is about 94%. That means that water wants to move from the outside of the cell (diluted) into the cell (more concentrated) to balance things. The urge water has to move is called hydroelectric power. That's the same electrical power generated at hydroelectric dams (like Hoover Dam). The energy make-up in your body is in part hydroelectric. I just know you wouldn't mind a little boost in energy.

Eat Smaller Amounts More Frequently ...become a 'grazer'

Eating a smaller amount reduces the stress of digestion on your energy supply. Eating small meals conserves energy. Give your energy generator a chance to keep up with digestion by not overwhelming it with a large meal. (The average meal time in the United States is 15 minutes. In Europe, the average meal time is 1 to 1½ hours. Little wonder Americans suffer such a high rate of digestive disorders.) When digestion is impaired, yeast overgrowth, gas, inflammation, food reactions, etc., are the results.

Another reason for eating smaller meals is to prevent the ups and downs of your blood sugar level, so you end up craving less sugar. As mentioned earlier, you can overwhelm your digestive capacity. You can also overwhelm your body's ability to handle sugar in the blood. Since the body will not (or should not) allow the blood sugar level to get too high, insulin and other hormones are secreted to lower the blood sugar. Often times, the insulin response is too strong and, within a short period of time, insulin has driven the blood sugar level down. As a result of low blood sugar, you get a powerful craving for sugar or other carbohydrates. You then usually overeat, and the cycle of ups and downs continues, resulting in yo-yo blood sugar results (depression and the lack of energy are all part of this cycle). Eating a small meal again will virtually stop this cycle.

Eating smaller meals also has advantages for your immune response to ingested food. It turns out that a small amount of food enters the blood without first going through the normal digestive pathway through the liver. As a result, this food is seen by the body not as nourishment, but as a threat and you will stimulate an immune reaction. Normally, a small immune reaction is not even noticed, but if a large amount of food is eaten (or if a food is eaten over and over again) the immune reaction can cause symptoms. Over time, disease develops.

By eating smaller amounts, the size of the reaction that occurs is small and inconsequential. A large meal, and thus a large assault of the immune system, could cause many symptoms of an activated immune system including fatigue, joint aches, flu-like symptoms, headaches, etc... This reaction was called the Metabolic Rejectivity Syndrome by the late nutritional pioneer Arthur L. Kaslow, M.D. Through thousands of his patients' food diaries, he compiled a list of high risk foods that is much the same as Dr. Page's.

Important Note:

Each of your meals *must* include some protein. The easiest sources are meat, fish, poultry, or eggs. (Count two eggs as equal to 3 oz). Vegetarians must combine proteins carefully and consistently using a different calculation. An easy way to calculate the amount of protein you need is to divide your ideal body weight by 15 to get the number of ounces of protein to be consumed per day. This is not a "high protein diet." Like many people, you already eat this much protein during a day, but you eat it mostly in one or two meals instead of spreading it out evenly over three to five meals. If you are more physically active, eat more protein. The following chart shows how much protein you will be allowed if you eat from three to five meals a day

90 lb. IBW = 6 ounces a day or 1 ¾ - 2 ounces of protein per serving
105 lb. IBW = 7 ounces a day or 1 ¾ - 2 $^1/_3$ ounces of protein per serving
120 lb. IBW = 8 ounces a day or 2 - 2 ¾ ounces of protein per serving
135 lb. IBW = 9 ounces a day or 2 ½ - 3 ounces of protein per serving
150 lb. IBW = 10 ounces a day or 3 - 3 $^1/_3$ ounces of protein per serving
165 lb. IBW = 11 ounces a day or 3 $^1/_3$ – 3 ¾ ounces of protein per serving
180 lb. IBW = 12 ounces a day or 3 ¾ - 4 ounces of protein per serving
195 lb. IBW = 13 ounces a day or 4 - 4 $^1/_3$ ounces of protein per serving

YEAST PROTOCOL

This protocol is used for patients struggling with Candida Albicans overgrowth.

Yeast overgrowth (Candida Albicans) is potentially a serious issue. Much has been written (Yeast Connection) that touts Candida as the culprit behind many ills. This may or may not be true. However, Candida is an opportunistic organism that grows rapidly if given the perfect condition and may be the cause of many problems.

Some reasons one gets Candida overgrowth:

1. Use of antibiotics – antibiotics kill off all the antagonists for Candida and allow the yeast to grow like crazy. Greatest defense – attempt at all costs to NOT take antibiotics. If needed, take an Acidophilus/Bifidus supplement along with it.
2. Other medications and surgeries

Ways to re-florize the gut (get the good, needed nutrients back):

1. Take Acidophilus orally through tablets, powder, capsules. (1-3/day)
2. Take Acidophilus mixed in an organic, raw yogurt – open a capsule and mix into yogurt, leave to sit on counter 30-45

minutes, eat/drink, swishing around in mouth so some can be absorbed through bucal mucosa (skin of cheeks). (1-3/day)
3. Women can mix Acidophilus with plain yogurt, water down and douche with it. This same liquid/mixture recipe can be used in an enema for both men and women.

***The idea is to get this Acidophilus into as many orifices as possible so your body may absorb as much as possible.

Your Body can't live without Glutathione

All autoimmune patients need increased glutathione. The problem is that oral consumption doesn't absorb well. We use nebulized glutathione in our office and have patients use a glutathione cream from Apex Energetics called Oxicell that absorbs directly through the skin and into the bloodstream.

You can now have a naturally occurring substance that acts as a powerful antioxidant, immune system balancer, and a detoxifier. Glutathione can help your body repair damage caused by stress, pollution, radiation, infection, drugs, poor diet, aging, injury, trauma and burns.

What is Glutathione? Also called GSH, Glutathione is the most powerful, prevalent antioxidant in your body. The most well known antioxidants are vitamins C and E. Glutathione is a tripeptide molecule composed of the amino acids glutamic acid, cysteine and glycine, which exists in almost every cell of your body. Our glutathione level actually indicates our state of health and can predict longevity. Scientific evidence has found that glutathione is needed by our body to enhance the immune system response. There are more than 60,000 published papers on the beneficial effects of glutathione replacement; unfortunately, it is still largely ignored by mainstream medicine. Normal glutathione levels are important for good health because they **neutralize free radicals**, which can build up in cells and cause damage.

The Bad News... Your body's cellular supply of glutathione begins to decline 10% to 15% per **decade** beginning with the age of 20. If you are over age 20, you have a glutathione shortage! Lower levels of glutathione can result in **chronic illness** such as; lowered energy or fatigue, a weakened immune system, cellular damage, accelerated aging, and higher cellular inflammation, which results in increased muscle and joint aches and pains. Free radicals constantly are attacking our cells, which is why antioxidants are so vital to protecting our health. Glutathione has been called the World's Most Powerful Antioxidant, and is found in every cell in the body, but, most people need some help.

The Good News! Research shows that increasing your Glutathione levels has the following benefits:

- **Increase Your Energy**
- **Slow Down the Aging Process**
- **Detoxify Your Body, Improve Liver Function**
- **Reduce the Risk of Cancer -Strengthen Your Immune System**
- **Improve Mental Function, Clarity -Fight Inflammation on Organs and Muscles**
- **Improve Heart / Lung Function**

Uncontrolled inflammation is a root cause of most major health issues ranging from heart conditions to joint and muscular conditions. Abundant glutathione levels will off-set the effects of this inflammation at the cellular level. Because glutathione is in every cell, it can regulate inflammation throughout the body.

Your Brain CRAVES FAT

Did you know that your brain is about 60 percent fat? The fats you eat strongly influence your level of brain function. Some nutritional anthropologists believe the human brain would not have developed as it did without access to high levels of DHA (a type of fat) found in fish and wild game. Just two generations of high omega-6 and low omega-3 fats can lead to profound changes in brain size and function.

Back in the 1930's, a dentist named Dr. Weston Price traveled throughout the South Pacific, examining traditional diets and their effect on dental and overall health. He found that **those eating diets high in coconut products were healthy and trim**, despite the high fat concentration in their diet.

Similarly, in 1981, researchers studied populations of two Polynesian atolls. Coconut was the chief source of caloric energy in both groups. The results, published in the *American Journal of Clinical Nutrition*, demonstrated that both populations exhibited positive vascular health.

There was no evidence that the high saturated fat intake had a harmful effect in these populations.

1. **Use Butter (Raw is best) or Coconut oil (solid at room temp) as a spread. You obviously cannot use butter if you have a dairy allergy or are autoimmune to casein.**
2. **Use Coconut oil to fry with and Olive oil to cook and bake with**
3. **Take 2 tsp Coconut oil per day orally**
4. **Take Omega-3 capsules every day**

Coconut Oil -- Your Smart Alternative to Those Other Oils

Coconut oil is finally beginning to get the respect it deserves as a smart alternative to other oils. The many benefits of GOOD FATS are finally reaching the mainstream:

- **Promoting your heart health – YES, good fats are good for your heart**
- Promoting weight loss when and if you need it – good fat makes you full
- **Supporting your immune system health – Th1 and Th2 response**
- Supporting a healthy metabolism – which helps regulate weight issues
- **Providing you with an immediate energy source**
- Helping to keep your skin healthy and youthful looking – you can rub Coconut oil on your skin as well!
- **Supporting the proper functioning of your thyroid gland AND Hormones**
- <u>**Good fats HEAL your brain and your cell membranes**</u>

Brain Based Therapy

Brain Based Therapy (BBT) is an amazingly powerful, all natural healing technique used to restore people to their optimum state of health. Antigens responsible for creating autoimmune conditions are attracted to fatty tissue. Fat cells have the spiritual gift of accommodation; they invite everyone over to dinner. Toxins that circulate in the blood are prone to settle in the fat surrounding the organs, gut and joint capsules. The brain and nervous system is all made up of fat and fatty acids, making it a prime target for toxins and autoimmune problems.

An antigen that has settled in the brain, midbrain, cerebellum, etc. is particularly hazardous to the autoimmune patient. Anxiety, depression, ASD (ADD/ADHD, OCD, Asperger's, and autism), Panic Attacks and learning disabilities are just a few of the diagnoses someone would be labeled with autoimmune responses against the frontal lobes. Dizziness, instability, unclear thoughts and early dementia are all tied to autoimmune cerebellum. Whenever there are autoimmune reactions that either directly (as those listed above) or indirectly affect the brain, Brain Based Therapy is an extremely useful tool to rehab pathways that are causing a world of symptoms.

How does the brain work?
Your brain controls and coordinates all function of the body (Grey's Anatomy). When functioning normally, the cerebellum, which is the back bottom part of your cranium, sends messages or "fires" to the brain (right and left hemisphere) which in turn "fires" to the brain stem (mesencephalon, pons, and medulla). This is called the "Brain Loop".

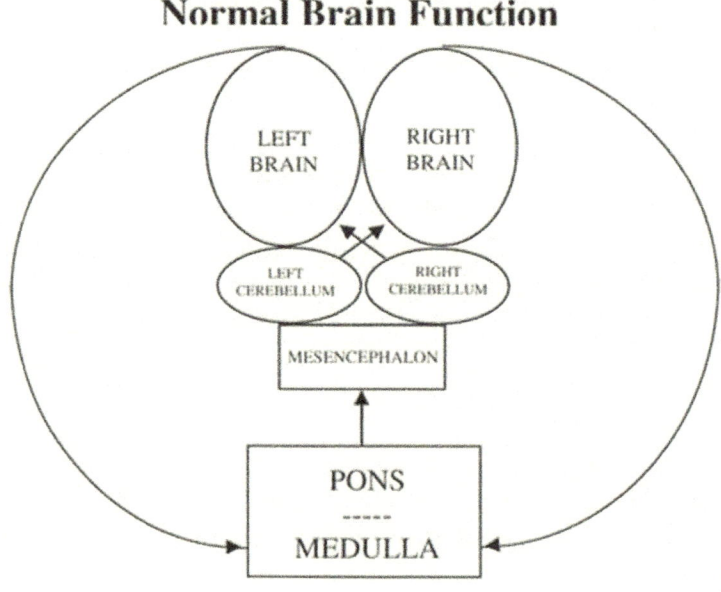

Your health, well-being, physical vitality, mental clarity, and emotional stability are all directly correlated with proper brain function... the "Brain Loop".

When functioning correctly, the cerebellum receives adequate input, sending normal input to the brain's frontal lobes, which sends sufficient input to the lower brainstem, keeping the mesencephalon, part of the midbrain, from over-firing.

What goes wrong?

Stress – physical, chemical, and emotional stress will adversely affect this "brain loop". Stress is not necessarily a bad thing. However, it is the constant, pervasive, never-ending stress of our culture that is so detrimental.

Abnormal Brain Function

If one side of the cerebellum is not receiving enough nerve input, it cannot send sufficient nerve input to the frontal lobe, which can't send enough input to the lower brainstem to keep the midbrain from over-firing.

What's the deal with the mesencephalon and the rest of the midbrain?

The mesencephalon (a.k.a. upper brain stem, a.k.a. midbrain, a.k.a. cerebral peduncle) normally is inhibited by the brain. In other words, when the "brain loop" is intact, the mesencephalon is turned off (or on low).

However, once stress interrupts the "brain loop", the mesencephalon is left unchecked. Basically, the brain gets stuck in a sympathetic (fight or flight) response.

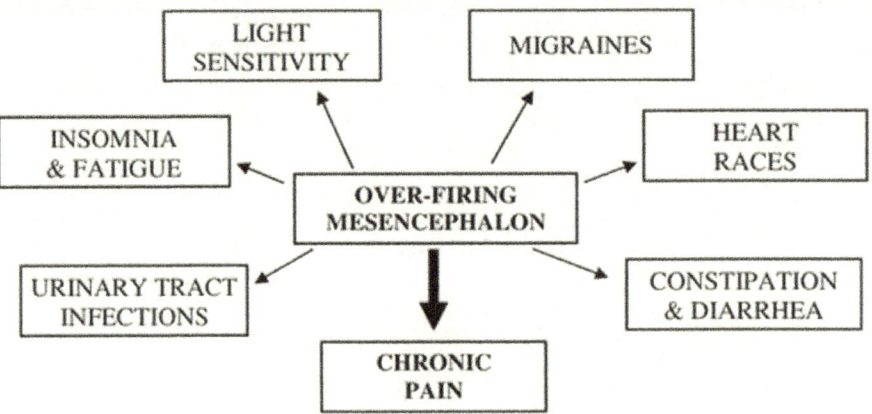

A mesencephalon that is not firing properly causes symptoms such as fibromyalgia, ADD, sciatica, etc.

What about the cerebellum?

Another key part to the "brain loop" is the cerebellum. This is the back, bottom part of your brain that controls your balance and coordination, spinal postural muscles, and terminates eye movements. When one side of your cerebellum is not firing properly it can lead to a host of common ailments.

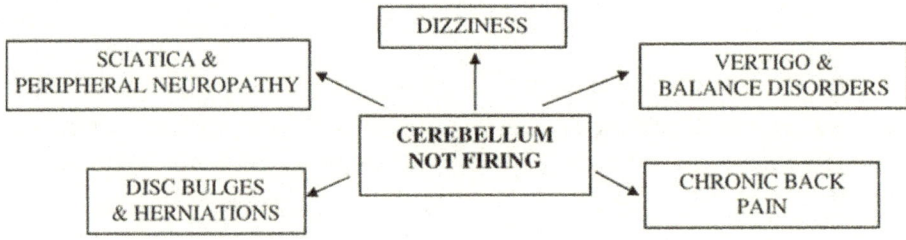

A mis-firing cerebellum will cause one side of the postural muscles to be in constant spasm. This one-sided muscle spasm will cause imbalances in the spinal bones. Additionally, individual vertebrae will lock up and be restricted in their normal movement. Consequently, chronic back and neck pain, spinal degeneration, arthritis, disc herniations, and sciatica may develop. Once pathologies are ruled out, chronic dizziness and balance disorders are usually the result of cerebellar dysfunction.

How do you fix the brain?

A thorough Brain Based Therapy neurological examination will reveal which aspect of your brain is not firing properly. Since once side of the body is controlled by the opposite side of the brain (example: right brain controls the left side of the body), most treatments are given on one side of the body to stimulate the opposite hemisphere of the brain.

A safe, gentle, hands-on, dynamic integration process is used to re-boot, reconnect and restore proper brain function. Traditional chiropractic instruments and/or adjustments are also used, but they are used in a very precise manner – to stimulate function in the effected part of the brain.

In addition, visual, auditory, and olfactory stimulation, heat, eye movements, eye exercises, and other modalities may be used to increase brain firing. Please understand that Brain Based Therapy is not a specific treatment for any disease, illness or disorder. We do not try to cure anything. Our expertise lies in naturally and holistically re-wiring your brain and then getting out of the way so your body can heal. However, once the "brain loop" is restored and any brain imbalances are minimized – amazing things can happen. The following is a list of health conditions people have shown significant improvement with:

- Balance disorders
- arm/shoulder pain
- low back pain/sciatica
- bulging/herniated discs
- carpal tunnel syndrome
- dizziness
- dystonia
- early Alzheimer's symptoms
- fibromyalgia
- RLS (restless leg syndrome)
- headaches
- migraines
- insomnia
- hip/knee/feet pain
- tremor disorders
- MS symptoms
- neck pain
- numbness
- Spinal Stenosis
- low immunity

Who discovered Brain Based Therapy?

Brain Based Therapy is a clinical, functional neurological protocol developed by Dr. Fred Carrick, the country's leading chiropractic neurologist and chiropractic's only Neurological Fellow. The Carrick Institute offers classes internationally and helps patients around the world with severe neurological disorders.

In addition, Dr. Michael Johnson, is a board certified chiropractic neurologist, and author of the best selling alternative health book, "What Do You Do When the Medications Don't Work?" He has developed a BBT/Neurological program for chiropractic neurologists in the United States who wish to pursue this expensive, post graduate training. We have been working closely with both Dr. Carrick and Dr. Johnson to ensure that the patients at our office can benefit from this amazing approach to overall health.

Take a look at our testimonials on our websites as well as the ones at www.lifechangingcare.com and see how our clinic and hundreds of other clinics across the country are using BBT to help people get out of chronic pain and change their lives!

Glossary

ASD/ADD/ADHD/Asperger's: Disorders within the Autism Spectrum often have an autoimmune connection. Autoimmune disease commonly affects the frontal lobes of the brain, the place of imbalance in ASD patients.

AIDS: Acquired Immune Deficiency Syndrome. HIV virus invades the T4 lymphocytes and multiplies, causing a breakdown in the body's immune system, leading to infection, cancer, autoimmune diseases.

A.I.D.P. Acute (sudden onset) Inflammatory Demyelinating Polyradiculoneuropathy

A.I.O.N. Anterior Ischemic Optic Neuropathy, loss of vision due to inflammation in posterior ciliary artery circulation in the optic nerve head.

Anaerobic: Of, relating to, or being an activity in which the body incurs an oxygen debt (for example weight training or resistive exercises) and does not immediately burn off a lot of calories and fat.

Anti-inflammatory: Reducing inflammation by acting on body mechanisms, without directly acting on the cause of inflammation, e.g., glucocorticoids, aspirin. Fish Oil

Anxiety/Depression: Patients with anxiety and/or depression should always be checked for autoimmune disorders. The frontal lobes of the brain as well as the autonomic centers in the midbrain are common attacks of an antigen.

Autoantibodies: Autoantibodies are Y shaped proteins that attack specific proteins or other substances found in specific tissues or organs of the body. They are created by the immune system when it fails to distinguish between "self" and "non-self." (They can be called the bad antibodies, e.g. "antinuclear antibody",).

Autoimmune Disease: One of a large group of diseases in which the immune system turns against the body's own cells, tissues and organs, leading to chronic inflammation and often serious conditions.

Autonomic failure or dysautonomia develops when the small nerves controlling heart rate, blood pressure, bowel movements, and skin color and hair integrity get involved with disease. Patients either have low blood pressure or high blood pressure, heart rate slow or fast. Often caused by autoimmune disease that is attacking the autonomic centers, the midbrain, baroreceptors, and frontal lobes must be accessed for antigens.

Axonal *degeneration,* called the "dying-back" phenomenon, results in axonal degeneration at the most far end of the axon of the nerves. Axonal degenerative polyneuropathies are usually symmetric, and as the disorder progresses, the axons typically degenerate from toes toward hands. Axonal degeneration is often attributed to a "metabolic" etiology which is commonly linked to autoimmune disease.

C.D.C. Center of Disease Control in the U.S.A. which issues disease alerts.

Cyanocobalamine: Vitamin B12 an essential vitamin not made by our body; this is a common type of anemia with autoimmune patients.

Bacteria: Microscopic germs. Some bacteria are "harmful" and can cause disease, while other "friendly" bacteria protect the body from harmful invading organisms. The bacteria that pose a threat to become antigens in an autoimmune condition are those that have the ability to 'wall themselves off' in the presence of an immune attack. Lymes Disease is a good example, killed easily within the first few weeks of onset, it later is impervious to antibiotic medications.

Borrelia burgdorferi: a Spirochete which causes Lymes Disease has world wide distribution. Symptoms of Lymes disease vary, and may not appear until 6–8 weeks after the tick bite, the infection is difficult to diagnose.

Bronchitis: Inflammation of the mucous membrane of the bronchial tubes, frequently accompanied by cough, hyper-secretion of mucus, and expectoration of sputum. Acute bronchitis is usually caused by an infectious agent. Chronic bronchitis the result of smoking, is **Chronic Obstructive Pulmonary Disease** (COPD) or **Emphysema**.

Cancer: Refers to the various types of malignant neoplasms that contain cells growing out of control and invading adjacent tissues, which may metastasize to distant tissues. Cancer is a common outcome of chronic autoimmune conditions since the hyper-immune response is inflammatory and chokes off nutrition and waste lines leading to cell mutation.

Candidiasis: Infection of the skin with any species of candida, usually *Candida albicans*. The infection is usually localized to the skin, nails, mouth, vagina, bronchi, or lungs, but may invade the bloodstream. It is a common inhabitant of the GI tract. Growth is encouraged by a weakened immune system, or with the prolonged use of antibiotics. Vaginal **symptoms** include itching, pain when urinating, and vaginal discharge.

C.N.S: Central Nervous System (Brain and spinal cord).

Chronic: Usually Chronic illness: Illness extending over a long period of time.

Ciliary: Often Ciliary activity: Activity of the eyelashes or any hair-like processes (cilia), like those found in the intestinal walls to increase the surface area for absorption.

Cold agglutinins: are abnormal proteins in the blood. They act as antibodies, causing red blood cells to clump together and die prematurely — especially at temperatures colder than normal body temperature

CRP: C-REACTIVE PROTEIN a test that measures autoimmune disease activity (0 is normal)

C.T. scan: Computed tomography scan makes pictures of the body by using x-rays and a computer.

Cytokines: Are chemical messengers that control immune responses. Secreted by white blood cells, T cells, and epithelial cells. There are at least 17 different kinds of interlukens and 3 classes of interferon called alpha, beta and gamma and various subsets. Interlukens and interferons are called "cytokines" and different ones will be increased in a Th1 response than those increased in a Th2 response.

Demyelination refers to focal loss of the **myelin** (outer nerve sheath) sheath with sparing of the axon (central fibers in the nerve). This reaction can be seen in focal mononeuropathies (single nerve injury) or generalized sensorimotor or predominantly motor neuropathies. Demyelination in the brain and spinal cord causes Multiple Sclerosis and in the peripheral nerves it causes (CIDP). Also called white matter disease.

D.H.E.A. A precursor hormone of testosterone. Used in the treatment of Chronic Fatigue & anti-ageing.

Diabetes: Type 1, or early onset diabetes is now thought to be an autoimmune disease and should be treated as one. Type 2, adult onset diabetes is most common and successfully treated with functional medicine. Diabetes is a state where there are increased blood glucose levels due to lack of effectiveness of insulin due to cell membrane receptor site down-regulation.

E.E.G. Electro Encephalographic Recording is a test to record electrical brain waves to help diagnose Epilepsy, sleep disorders and brain death.

E.S.R. test used to measure inflammation, infection (10 – 15 mm is normal) also called **Sedimentation rate or sed rate**

Fibromyalgia: (FMS): An autoimmune disease affecting the fascia and muscles causing pain and stiffness in multiple locations.

F.D.A: Food and Drug Administration (agency monitoring safety of new drugs through drug trials) The treatment guidelines of FDA are followed by physicians, governments all over the World.

G.B.S. Guillain-Barre Syndrome, sudden or slow onset of weakness after flu due to autoimmune disease.

Gingivitis: Inflammation of the fibrous tissues that surround the teeth.

Glucose: A sugar that is the simplest form of carbohydrate, serves as the primary fuel for the muscles and the brain.

HAART: A multi drug therapy for treatment of AIDS.

HIV: Human immunodeficiency virus which causes AIDS.

Hormones: Chemical secreted by body organs are carried by the bloodstream and influence cells some distance from the source of production. Examples: adrenal hormones such as corticosteroids and aldosterone; glucagon, growth hormone, insulin, testosterone, estrogens, progesterone, DHEA, melatonin, and thyroid hormones.

Horners: Horner syndrome is a small pupil (miosis), droopy eyelid (ptosis), and shrunken eyeball (enophthalmos) and reduction of sweating on the ipsilateral side of the face and neck,; occasionally the development of cataracts; same side loss of sweating (hemifacial anhidrosis) .

H.S.P. Heat shock proteins, or *stress proteins*, are a group of proteins that are present in all cells in all life forms. They are induced when a cell undergoes environmental stresses like heat, cold and oxygen deprivation.

I.C. Interstitial cystitis a bladder infection induced autoimmune disorder

Immune System: A complex that protects the body from disease organisms and other foreign bodies.

Irritable Bowel Syndrome: (IBS) is inflammation of intestines with pain in the lower abdomen; bloating, alternating diarrhea and constipation; mucous in stools; indigestion; constant tiredness; low back pain; painful intercourse in women.

I.V.I.G. Intra Venous Immune Globulin a solution containing IgG antibodies from Humans.

Leukemia: Cancer of the lymph glands and bone marrow resulting in overproduction of white blood cells (related to Hodgkin's disease).

Leukocyte: A white blood cell which appears 5,000 to 10,000 times in each cubic millimeter of normal human blood. Among the functions are destroying bacteria, fungi and viruses and rendering harmless poisonous substances.

Lymes disease caused by a spirochete called **Borrelia burgdorferi.** First recognized in the United States, following a mysterious outbreak of juvenile rheumatoid arthritis near the community of Lymes, Connecticut, Lymes disease is an autoimmune, systemic attack on various joints and organs.

Metabolism: The chemical processes of living cells in which energy is produced Responsible for the production of energy, biosynthesis of important substances, and degradation of various compounds.

Mold: Molds are Fungi which produce allergens (substances that can cause allergic reactions), irritants, and in some cases, potentially toxic substances (mycotoxins). Inhaling or touching mold or mold spores may cause allergic reactions in sensitive patients. Allergic responses include sneezing, runny nose, red eyes, and skin rash.

Myelin: Wrapping around the nerve fibers, Myelin conduct electrical impulses faster.

M.R.I. Magnetic resonance imaging scan used to make pictures of the body by using magnets with a computer.

MTHFR stands for **M**ethylene-**T**etra-**H**ydro-**F**olate-**R**eductase. MTHFR is an enzyme it is needed to metabolize and get rid of homocysteine. High homocysteine levels are a risk factor for blood clots in the veins or arteries. Levels of homocysteine can be lowered by taking a multiple vitamin with a high content of folic acid and the B vitamins.

N.I.H. National Institutes of Health (Medical Research Agency in USA)

O.C.D. Obsessive-compulsive disorder is an autoimmune psychiatric disorder stemming from a frontal lobe problem. It often has an autoimmune link.

Parasite: An organism living in or on another organism.

PFOA stands for Perfluorooctanoic Acid, a man-made chemical. PFOA (sometimes also called "C8") is used by companies, such as DuPont (Teflon, Stainmaster, Scotchguard), to make fluoro-polymers for use in non-stick cookware and all-weather clothing. PFOA have been commonly found in humans across the globe.

Pyelonephritis: Inflammation of the renal pelvis.

Raynaud's syndrome is a disorder of blood circulation in the fingers. Exposure to cold reduces blood circulation causing the fingers to become pale, white or purple. Raynaud's most commonly associated with hand-arm vibration

Rickettsia: Bacteria, are carried by many ticks, fleas, and lice, and cause diseases such as typhus, rickettsialpox, Rocky Mountain spotted fever, Like viruses, they grow only in living cells.

Rituximab: The first monoclonal antibody therapy approved in the United States for the treatment of relapsed or refractory non-Hodgkin's lymphoma (NHL).

E.S.R. Erythrocyte Sedimentation Rate is used to measure inflammation, infection (10 – 15 mm is normal)

Syndrome number of symptoms described together, Example; dry eyes and dry mouth is Sjogrens syndrome.

Tilt Test: People with syncope are placed on a Tilt table and their blood pressure and pulse is monitored. If the person gets symptoms or the blood pressure falls after standing up then the test is considered positive.

TMJ: Tempero-mandibular joint of the jaw, often a site of autoimmune attack.

Urea breath test Is a procedure for diagnosing the presence of a bacterium, Helicobacter pylori (H. pylori) that causes inflammation, ulcers, and atrophy of the stomach. This is the most reliable test for H. Pylori infections.

Virus: A small bug with a DNA and/or RNA that reproduces in the cells of the infected host.

White Blood Cell: (WBC): A blood cell also called as leukocyte that does not contain hemoglobin and is responsible for maintaining the body's immune surveillance system against invasion by foreign media.

White Matter Disease: caused by destruction of Myelin in the Brain, in Multiple Sclerosis or outside the brain in CIDP (loss of myelin in nerves). Please also see under demyelination.

Special thanks to:

Dr. Datis Kharrazian, DC, DHS, MS, MNeuroSci, FAACP, DACBN, DABCN, DIBAK, CNS, Author, Lecturer, Author of "Why Do I Still Have Thyroid Symptoms?" www.thyroidbook.com

Dr. Michael Johnson, DC, DACBN, Lecturer, Author of "What to Do When Your Medications Don't Work"

Dr. Imran Khan M D (MBBS)
Board Certified Neurology and Psychiatry, Fellow of National Institutes of Health USA.
Contact me through www.cidpusa.org Dr. Imran Khan Nanotech Neurology Lahore

Dr. George John Georgiou
Clinical Nutrition (Dip.ION) from the Institute of Optimum Nutrition (ION), London, England; diplomas in Naturopathy, Medical Herbalism (M.H.) and Iridology (R.Ir.,MRNI) from the Holistic Health College, London, UK; and a Diploma in Electronic Impulse Therapy (Dip.E.I.Th) from the Euro College of Complementary Medicine, UK. He has also been awarded a Diploma in Homeopathic Medicine (DIHom.) from the British Institute of Homeopathy, Middlesex, England. He has a Licentiate Diploma in Chinese Acupuncture (L.Dip.Ac.,aM.A.C.Ac.-TCMI) from the College of Oriental Medicine, UK and the Cyprus Acupuncture Institute; and is a qualified Su Jok Acupuncturist. www.detoxmetals.com

Apex Energetics Nutrition – this is the gluten-free, soy-free, and casein-free supplement line we use and I highly recommend.

Contact us at:

Dr. Kevin Conners
Dr. Mallory Ranem

Upper Room wellness center
1654 East County Road E
Vadnais Heights, MN 55110
651.739.1248

www.upperroomwellness.com
www.takemypain.com
www.AmIAutoimmune.com
www.curemybrain.com
www.curemyADHD.com

Made in United States
Orlando, FL
17 January 2023